To Simon and Mindy.
Yeidiklatsók Ḵaa Ḵaahání
Chíok
Shangukéidí
Lukaax̱.ádi Yádi
Kaadli ayahéet
Chilḵát Ḵwaan

CELEBRATION

Tlingit, Haida, Tsimshian *Dancing on the Land*

ROSITA WORL

With a Foreword by BYRON I. MALLOTT *and essays*
by MARIA WILLIAMS *and* ROBERT DAVIDSON
Edited by KATHY DYE
Principal photography by BILL HESS

Published by SEALASKA HERITAGE INSTITUTE, Juneau, Alaska
in association with UNIVERSITY OF WASHINGTON PRESS, Seattle and London

© 2008 by Sealaska Heritage Institute
All rights reserved. No part of this publication may be reproduced or transmitted in any form or by any means, electronic or mechanical, including photocopy, recording, or any information storage or retrieval system, without permission in writing from the publisher.

SEALASKA HERITAGE INSTITUTE
One Sealaska Plaza, Suite 301
Juneau, Alaska 99801
907.463.4844
www.sealaskaheritage.org

UNIVERSITY OF WASHINGTON PRESS
P.O. Box 50096, Seattle, WA 98145 U.S.A.
www.washington.edu/uwpress

SEALASKA HERITAGE INSTITUTE BOARD OF TRUSTEES
Dr. Walter Soboleff, Chair
Marlene Johnson, Vice-Chair
Joe Nelson, Secretary
Nancy Barnes
Jeane Breinig
William Demmert
Clarence Jackson
Ethel Lund
Robert Martin

LIBRARY OF CONGRESS CATALOGING-IN-PUBLICATION DATA
Worl, Rosita.
Celebration : Tlingit, Haida, Tsimshian dancing on the land / Rosita Worl ; with foreword by Byron I. Mallott and essays by Maria Williams and Robert Davidson ; edited by Kathy Dye ; principal photography by Bill Hess.
   p. cm.
ISBN 978-0-295-98829-0 (hardback : alk. paper)
1. Tlingit Indians—Social life and customs.
2. Haida Indians—Social life and customs.
3. Tsimshian Indians—Social life and customs.
I. Williams, Maria (Maria P.)
II. Davidson, Robert, 1946–
III. Dye, Kathy. IV. Sealaska Heritage Institute.
V. Title.
E99.T6W67 2008
305.897'07982—dc22   2007051446

The paper used in this publication meets the minimum requirements of American National Standard for Information Sciences—Permanence of Paper for Printed Library Materials, ANSI Z39.48-1984.

Project management and editorial services:
Suzanne G. Fox, Red Bird Publishing, Inc., Bozeman, Montana
Graphic design: Carol Beehler, Bethesda, Maryland
Printer: Asia Pacific Offset
Tlingit words edited by Keri Edwards
Haida words edited by Jordan Lachler

PHOTO CREDITS
All photographs in this book were made by Bill Hess, except the following: Brown Bear Clan Hat, photo by Mark Kelley, page 36; Early tourist masks, photo by Mark Kelley, page 44; Thank You Halibut People, photo by Chloe French, page 132; Tsirku River Robe, photo by Lani Hotch, page 132; The Good Book, photo by Nicholas Galanin, page 133; Raven Rattle, photo by Russell Johnson, Seattle, page 134; Fooled You Again, photo by Mark Kelley, page 134; Copper Woman; Raven *Shakee.át*, photos by Mark Kelley, page 135; Raven's Dream, photo by Dr. William Pfeifer, page 135; Jeanine, photo by Deborah Head, page 136.; Killerwhale earrings, photo by Richard Beasley, page 136; Black seaweed, photo by Mark Kelley, page 138. The following photos are from Sealaska Heritage Institute's photo collection: Tlingit Movement, page 133; Chilkat doll, page 136; Keeper of the Halibut, Potlatch spoon, Moccasins, page 137.

Front cover: Grand exit, 2004.
Back cover: Baby Regalia Review. Kaden Dean Jim.
Page 1: Mt. Saint Elias Dancers. Left to right: Marie Shodda, Tim Brown, Gloria Anderstrom, unidentified.
Frontispiece: Left to right, Felicia Daniels (wearing glasses), Pauline Jim (rear), Jeannette Kookesh holding a dragonfly rattle.

Printed in China

Contents

Foreword • **6**
Byron I. Mallott

Preface and Acknowledgments • **9**

Honoring Our Ancestors and Cultural Survival: A Retrospective View of Celebration • **15**

Art and *At.óow* • **37**

Tlingit Ceremonial Music and Dance: Survival and Adaptation • **61**
Maria Williams

Ceremonial Masks of the Tlingit, Haida, and Tsimshian • **101**

    Becoming the Mask • **114**
    Robert Davidson

Celebration Events • **121**

The Authors • **152**

Foreword

It is good that the Sealaska Heritage Institute hosts Celebration every two years on behalf of the Native Peoples of Southeast Alaska.

It is good that Sealaska Corporation created the Sealaska Heritage Institute so that the culture, languages, and traditions of Native Peoples may be celebrated and strengthened.

It is good that the Tlingit, Haida, and Tsimshian Peoples always remembered who they are and used their strength to keep some of their ancestral lands and demanded payment for that which they could not keep so that Sealaska Corporation could become the steward of those Native lands and the trustee of the money. It is good because all of this might not have been except for the strength and vision of Native Peoples.

There might not have been Celebration, for beginning with first contact with foreigners, Alaska's Natives were subjected to unremitting and often brutal crusades to rip from their very core the essence of their being. Language, dance, sustenance, spirituality, history, tradition, family, and community—all were assaulted in the name of fur, salmon, gold, government, and God. In the living memory of Native elders is the searing knowledge that these things truly happened, because they lived through them.

It is good that Native grandparents and those before them hung on passionately to all that defined them even as they bowed to the onslaught.

It is good that even as Native generations seemed to have given up all that made them who they are to live in their times, they deep inside remembered and quietly passed on to their children all that makes them Native People.

It is good that we remember, for if we forget, it could happen again. Not in the same way, but by the powerful and seductive attractions of modern times. These are times in which we must live and prosper, but we must never forget who we are as Native Peoples. And we must continue to Celebrate that knowledge and strengthen it.

For the times of the past when Native Peoples were forbidden to Celebrate, we must forgive, even if there has been no apology. For those who now Celebrate with us, we welcome you. For all of this Earth's people, we must Celebrate together.

It is good that we know deep in our spirit that Celebration will go on long beyond our time.

It is good that we know our children will know who they are.

BYRON I. MALLOTT
July 2007

Preface and Acknowledgments

I WAS PRIVILEGED to play a part in the first Celebration in 1982. As a member of the Alaska State Arts Council Traditional Native Artist Panel (TNAP), I had promoted the development of a grant program dedicated to regional cultural events and endangered arts. I also served on the Sealaska Heritage Foundation (now Sealaska Heritage Institute) Board of Trustees, which was awarded a TNAP grant to support the first Celebration. Concurrently with Celebration, we held a forum on Tlingit property law with a group of clan leaders, a Tlingit trained in Western law, and myself as the anthropologist. The trustees had been concerned that not all children had the opportunity to participate in traditional ceremonies and as a consequence were not learning our ancient songs and dances and other dimensions of our culture. At that time, I could not fathom the success that Celebration would achieve, or that Celebration would prompt the formation of dance groups throughout the region and grow to become the largest cultural event in the state.

Celebration is recorded each year through photographs, including a panoramic photo of all the dancers, and videotaped, providing us with an extensive visual history of the event. In 2000, Celebration was televised for the first time, bringing it into homes across the state. It was also available to an international audience through a webcast. We initially had some concern that the broadcast might deter folks from coming to Celebration. Our fear proved to be wrong. Some of those watching TV caught the excitement of Celebration

Naa Luudisk Gwaii Yátx'i (Children of the Islands Who Learn) of Anchorage.

and scurried to catch planes from Anchorage and elsewhere to Juneau. Others called the institute to express their approval and appreciation for the broadcast. Some who were watching Celebration from their homes in Juneau also felt the need to rush to Centennial Hall, the venue. Those living in the villages who could not send dancers to Celebration were gratified to participate even in this limited way. The broadcast brought Celebration into the homes of countless families throughout the world who had never seen traditional dance performances and gave them a glimpse of the vitality of our culture.

The Board of Trustees of Sealaska Heritage Institute has long wanted a book devoted to Celebration photographs. Celebration brings great joy to participants and observers throughout the year, long after Celebration has ended. Many watch videotapes and DVDs of past Celebrations to recapture the happy moments or to see friends and relatives. The trustees felt a book with Celebration photographs could enhance this benefit and be enjoyed throughout the year, and might even encourage readers to come to the next Celebration.

The difficulty in producing a book of a photographic collection is not that suitable photographs are not available, but rather in selecting photographs for the publication. Fortunately, SHI has contracted with talented photographers through the years to document Celebration, and we have an excellent collection. The agony comes in paring down the collection to 200 photographs. We indicated we wanted to have photographs representing every community, a sampling of elders, youngsters, dancers, and participants, as well as some Celebration events and activities. The Baby Regalia Review proved to be the most challenging, and in the end, we told the photographer and designers to try to include every child who entered the Baby Regalia Review. Of course, our lead photographer also had his own artistic needs in the selection of photographs.

The next major issue was trying to identify individuals in the photographs. We first circulated the photographs in Sealaska Heritage Institute and Sealaska Corporation offices. We pleaded with every visitor who came to our SHI office to review the photographs. We followed up on countless leads given to us by the reviewers, who gave us names of people who might know the yet un-named individuals featured in the photographs. Our final effort was to dispatch SHI Intern Neely Perisich, assisted by John Marks, to visit other Native offices to find the names of those who had not been identified in our first efforts. The process of trying to identify everyone featured in the photographs brought great joy as well as moments of sadness in seeing friends and relatives who had "Walked into the Forest," as we say in Southeast Alaska when someone has passed away. If individuals remain unnamed by the time of publication, we invite those who see the publication and who know the names of individuals to let our office know. In the event that another edition of the book is published, we will be able to add those names.

We also felt the need to include essays in the publication that would explain the cultural and historical context of Celebration, since we realized that not every reader would be familiar with the rich cultures of the Tlingit, Haida, and Tsimshian. The essays are intended to be introductions. They are offered in the hope that people might be encouraged to read further about these complex cultures.

The success of Celebration first and foremost must be attributed to the ancestors of the Tlingit, Haida, and Tsimshian who bequeathed to their descendants the values that have sustained their cultures through the centuries and through the difficult cultural encounters with Western societies. The elders were a significant force in prompting the initiation of Celebration. They had used the metaphor of a blanket symbolizing our culture and conveyed to the Sealaska leadership, "Our hands are growing weary of holding onto this blanket." They told Sealaska that they were passing the responsibility of educating our young to them. Sealaska accepted the challenge, and under the leadership of CEO Byron Mallott and its Board of Directors responded to the call to educate the younger generations of Native people. Their foresight must be applauded. Since the first Celebration, Sealaska has provided the core financial resources for Celebration. Even in times of financial stress, the corporation continued to provide funds for the event.

The Board of Trustees of Sealaska Heritage Institute must also be acknowledged. We thank David Katzeek, who served as the President of the Heritage Foundation, Judson

Brown, Chair of the Board of Trustees, and the Council of Elders for their guidance in directing the first Celebration. Because of the cultural complexities and sensitivities of integrating traditional practices into a new and secular event, the trustees delegated operational oversight responsibility to the Celebration Committee. The committee, under the leadership of Marlene Johnson, deserves great applause for making difficult decisions and balancing the needs of all participants.

Celebration, which has grown beyond a dance festival and now includes a multitude of activities, is an expensive endeavor. Without the financial support of Sealaska and a host of donors including the City of Juneau, the University of Alaska, the National Endowment for the Arts, and a number of individuals—notably Carolyn Kleefeld, who has contributed substantial funds through the years—Celebration might not be possible. Equally as significant are the dedicated volunteers and the staff of SHI, who work round the clock for the entire period to ensure a smooth running operation. We owe them a great debt.

The heart and success of Celebration are the dancers! They realized the great expense of Celebration and they agreed to support it, not only through their dance performances, but also through the fees they pay. The dance groups, some led by clan leaders or a dance leader, practice throughout the year to ready themselves for Celebration. We benefit from their dedication and perseverance, not only from the performances at Celebration, but also because they are instrumental in ensuring that the dances, songs, stories, and our ancient cultural practices are taught to the younger generation.

Insofar as this Celebration book goes, we owe a tribute to the Board of Trustees and its Chair, Dr. Walter Soboleff, who were unrelenting in their desire to have such a publication. Marlene Johnson, Chair of the Celebration Committee, who never let a meeting pass without mentioning a Celebration book, also greatly assisted in the production. Our featured photographer, Bill Hess, who provided us an historical record of our Celebration and whose creative talents are evident through the photographs, must be acknowledged. As our work was commencing, Bill continued to meet the tight production deadlines even as he was grieving the passing of his father. Kathy Dye, SHI's Media and Publications

Director who served as editor for this publication, maintained a calm demeanor through the entire process and gently prodded us all along to ensure that we could have the publication available by Celebration 2008. Suzanne G. Fox of Red Bird Publishing managed the project and kept us on course with her wise counsel. Carol Beehler applied her gift for creativity and delivered a design that exceeded expectations. Pat Soden and the University of Washington Press helped to guide the project through the final stages, continuing a long and mutually beneficial partnership with the institute. We owe a special tribute to the SHI and Sealaska staff and to the many others who assisted in identifying individuals featured in the photographs. We owe our greatest apologies to those featured in the photographs whom we were not able to identify.

Celebration has grown to mean so much more than a three-day dance festival. It is a time for cultural and family renewal. It is a time to reconnect with our past and our ancestors. It is a time to dance on our land and feel the ground beneath our feet. It is a time to watch the faces of our young and our future. We owe a debt to all who have contributed to Celebration. Dr. Soboleff aptly described the contribution of Celebration participants: "You have shared in the preservation of our culture!" ■

ROSITA WORL
Juneau, Alaska
January 2008

Honoring Our Ancestors and Cultural Survival
A Retrospective View of Celebration

ROSITA WORL

THE TLINGIT, HAIDA, AND TSIMSHIAN of Southeast Alaska developed one of the most complex societies in indigenous North America. Their rich cultural and artistic traditions were nourished by abundant natural resources from the seas and land. They boast of an occupation of Southeast Alaska "since time immemorial," and archaeological evidence attests to an indigenous presence for more than 10,000 years. With the intimate knowledge of the land gained through thousands of years of occupation, their highly organized socioeconomic groups, and a strong entrepreneurial sense, these Southeast Alaska Indians traveled thousands of miles to trade with their neighbors to the north and into the interior reaches of the continent as well as southward along the coasts of Washington and Oregon.

Following their ancient trading practices with the neighboring tribes, the Tlingit, Haida, and Tsimshian welcomed the commercial opportunities and the new material culture brought by Russians and other Europeans who arrived in their homeland beginning in 1741. Our ancestors asserted dominion over all the lands and waters of Southeast Alaska, and they could not fathom that the United States could claim ownership when it purchased Alaska from Russia in 1867. With the erosion of Native ownership and control over lands and resources and under the assimilative policies of the United States, it seemed

Austin Hammond, *Lukaax.ádi* (Sockeye) clan leader. 1984.

that Native cultures would succumb to the pressures of Western society. But Native people were determined to regain control of their land and their lives.

With an initial judicial settlement of their aboriginal land claims in 1968 and a congressional settlement in 1971, the Southeast Alaska Natives took greater control of their communities. The Central Council of Tlingit and Haida Indian Tribes of Alaska organized to provide government services to tribal constituents. Village corporations and a region-wide corporation, created to implement the congressional land claims settlement, eagerly pursued new economic opportunities.

Sealaska Corporation, the region-wide corporation, established the Sealaska Heritage Institute (initially the Sealaska Heritage Foundation) at the behest of clan leaders and elders. David Katzeek, the first president of the new organization, recalls that the elders believed educating the youth about their cultural heritage should be one of its foremost priorities. He recounts the words of one of the elders, George Davis: "One day, we'll be able to raise the Titanic and see the kind of artifacts that were in that vessel. But when we die, who will come to our graves and ask us about the culture, the language, the traditions and customs of our people? We need to let the people know this."

Perpetuating Native culture became the mission of the fledgling organization, and one of the first major functions was a region-wide gathering of clans to showcase their culture and *at.óow* (treasured clan objects). The elders and the Board of Trustees of Sealaska Heritage decided that the gathering would be similar to a traditional ceremonial *ḵu.éex'*, which translates "invite." In this secular and public event, participants were invited to celebrate their culture and honor their ancestors through traditional songs and dance.

The first Celebration, which was held in 1982, drew a couple of hundred people, mostly adults. Along with the dancing and singing, a group of traditional leaders and elders also met to outline the traditional property laws governing ownership of clan property. The festival reunited family members with those who had left their home communities and made a lasting impression on people. David Katzeek recalls an emotional event that took place at the first Celebration:

I'll never forget this one lady in high heels who walked down the middle of the hall so everyone could see her. She walked onstage and apologized for interrupting Clarence Jackson of Kake. She spoke about the people standing on the stage, and said, "This is my family. I have been away from Kake, and I want to thank Sealaska and Sealaska Heritage Foundation for having this event because I found my family." People had tears running down their faces. There was a lot of shouting and applause. It was a very powerful experience!

Children were notably absent, partly because the event was held during the school year. More likely, however, the contributing factor was that very few children were learning about their traditional culture. After the first festival, the leaders decided that Sealaska would continue to sponsor Celebration every other year. And, they decided to hold subsequent Celebrations in summer to encourage children to attend.

The first Celebration sparked a movement that took on a life of its own. Dance groups sprouted in every community. Children learned their ancient songs and dances. Mothers and grandmothers began to sew regalia in anticipation of the next Celebration rather than commissioning others to make their ceremonial regalia, which is the traditional practice. To support the event, dance groups decided that they would help offset the expense of Celebration by charging themselves a modest fee.

Celebration is now one of the largest events in the state, drawing more than forty dance groups from Southeastern Alaska communities, Anchorage, Seattle, Portland, and San Francisco, as well as Canadian Tlingit and Haida dance groups from the Yukon Territory and British Columbia. Additionally, guest groups from Hawaii or New Zealand have regularly attended since 1988. Traditionally, only clan members danced together in ceremonial activities. Although a few clans participate in Celebration, the greater majority of dance groups tend to be community-based groups whose members are from different Eagle and Raven clans. Additionally, the Haida and Tsimshian each formed dance groups. In contrast to the first festival, present-day Celebrations are well attended by children.

Opposite: **Grand entrance at Centennial Hall in Juneau. 2004.**

Celebration also has grown to include a host of other activities and has been extended from three to five days. Like the salmon returning to their home, tribal members return home to visit with their family and friends and to celebrate the cultural vitality of the Tlingit, Haida, and Tsimshian. Katzeek reminisces,

> Many of the Elders who sowed the seeds for the first Celebration are no longer with us, but I feel that much of what the elders wanted to happen has happened, and it's continuing to happen. I don't know whether we're raising the Titanic or whether we're going to a gravesite, but the language and culture materials developed by the Sealaska Heritage Institute are phenomenal. And Celebration has had a big impact on us as a people. The greatest contribution of Celebration is the recognition, acknowledgment and acceptance of ourselves and not being afraid to let people know who we are. We want our voices to sound across the land, and that's what happens at Celebration. Thousands come. And our voices ring across the land.

Celebration: Tlingit, Haida, Tsimshian Dancing on the Land is a photographic collection of the biennial dance festivals and activities held in Juneau, Alaska, since 1982. The book also contains essays that delineate the contextual framework of Celebration in music, dance, regalia, and traditional art. The authors are Native artists and academics, and thus readers will see such words as *ku.éex'* and *at.óow* in lieu of the English words for "potlatch" and "property." The English words fail to convey or embody Native concepts, and the Native words are used in the hopes of replacing some erroneous conceptions conveyed in earlier anthropological writings.

While Southeast Native societies have undergone dramatic transformations, elements of our cultures persist, although admittedly they differ from earlier traditional practices. We hope that this book will allow readers to participate in the joyous Celebrations and perhaps to recall family members and friends who "Walked into the Forest." We hope that some will relive the moments captured in these photographs.

Above: The first Celebration, 1982. Left to right, onstage: Mary Johnson wearing an Eagle blanket clasp, Sophie Marvin, Irene Lampe wearing sash, Kathryn Polk, unidentified, unidentified (boy), Reginald Dangeli holding a staff, William Jackson (face partially obscured), Jayne Dangeli (face obscured by drum), Anita Lafferty (rear, in profile), Carolyn Dangeli holding drum in the air, others unidentified. Offstage, left: Anna Katzeek (rear), Martha Katzeek wearing Chilkat robe.

Above right: Austin Hammond, *Lukaax̱.ádi* (Sockeye) clan leader. 1984.

Right: Reginald Dangeli holding a staff

20 • *Celebration*

Far left: Herman Kitka, *Kaagwaantaan* (Wolf) clan leader, Violet James.

Albert Davis, *L'uknax.ádi* (Coho) clan leader, wearing a Coho clan hat. 1984.

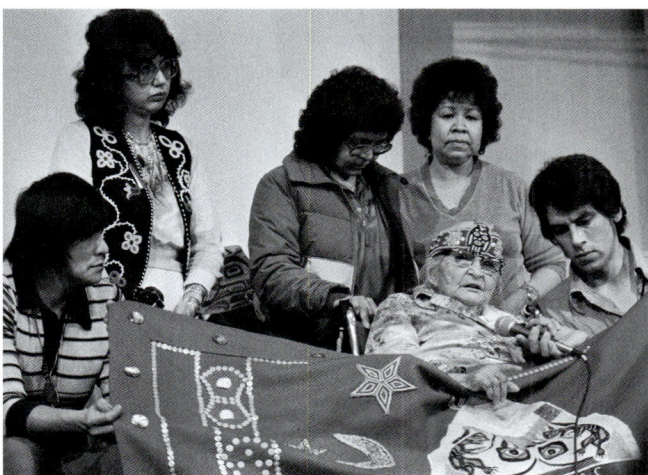

Far left: Matthew Fred, *Deisheetaan* (Beaver) clan leader, holding a Raven rattle. 1982.

Left to right: unidentified, Vicki Demmert, Jean Hogue, Maggie Adams wearing beaded headband, Emma Demmert, Albert Porter. 1982.

Honoring Our Ancestors and Cultural Survival • 21

Mary Katasse. 1984.

Opening ceremony with welcome by Clarence Jackson (center) with Rosita Worl, Dr. Walter Soboleff, *L'eeneidí* (Dog Salmon) clan leader, and Alaska Senator Albert Kookesh, Chair, Sealaska Board of Directors.

Top left: Left to right, front: Johnny Marks wearing Killer Whale bib and Eagle headdress, Elena Marie Topacio, Nora Dauenhauer wearing a Double-Headed Raven tunic and White Raven headband, Ronaldo Topacio. Left to right, rear: George Dalton, Dora Williams, Katherine Mills (against wall), Elsie Pratt (front), Sophie Marvin wearing headdress (rear), Mary Wilson, Al Martin, Amy Marvin. 1982.

Above: Left to right: Annie Joseph, Albert Davis, Mary Perkins, Vida Davis, Esther Littlefield. 1984.

Left: Opening ceremony with welcome by Alaska Senator Albert Kookesh, with Rosita Worl, President, Sealaska Heritage Institute.

Honoring Our Ancestors and Cultural Survival • 23

Left to right: Patti Paul, Jeff David, Dr. Walter Soboleff. 1982.

Dr. Walter Soboleff wearing a Dog Salmon clan hat and showing a Raven drum for the 2004 panoramic photo.

24 • *Celebration*

Above left: Left to right: Jeff David wearing Chilkat robe, Rachel Johnson (rear), Jennie Thlunaut (the last traditional Chilkat weaver), Brendan Winders, Agnes Bellinger. 1982.

Above: Clarence Jackson and Chris E. McNeil, President and CEO, Sealaska Corporation, placing a Sealaska Pendleton blanket on Peter Jack, *Teikweidí* (Brown Bear) clan leader, during a ceremony in 2006 to honor Jack's years of service to Native people. Looking on, Reanna Kookesh-Booth.

Left: Ira Booth (center) enjoying a humorous moment with two unidentified women. 1982.

Honoring Our Ancestors and Cultural Survival

Above: Children at the second Celebration. Although attendance by children was low at the early festivals, they comprise a large segment of participants today. Left to right: Raymond Paddock, unidentified, unidentified. 1984.

Above right: These unidentified dancers may be from Angoon and Haines. The boy in front is wearing a Beaver, which suggests Angoon. The boy behind him is wearing a *Deishú* (Haines) Dancers headband. 1984.

Right: Left to right, front: Nicole Horne, Aubrielle Horne. Left to right, rear: unidentified, Vincent Dundas, Sr. (center, holding drum), Aaron Horne.

Above: Left to right: Paul Marks, Carlton Smith, Robert Martin, Sr., Marlene Johnson, Jessica Sutherland, Judson Brown wearing a Killer Whale hat, David Katzeek, then-President of Sealaska Heritage Institute, wearing White Bear tunic, Robert Cogo, Dr. Walter Soboleff, Vicki Soboleff, unidentified, Erma Lawrence, unidentified. 1984.

Far right: Left to right: Charlie Joseph holding a staff showing Beaver with Frog in its mouth, William Nelson (rear), Kathryn Duncan (face obscured), Jimmie George, Lydia George. In the foreground is a *Ch'áak'* (Eagle) hat, *at.óow* worn by David Katzeek, *Shangukweidí* (Thunderbird) clan leader. 1982.

Right: Left to right, front: Mary Wilson, Amy Marvin. 1982.

Top left: Dancers from Metlakatla performing with paddles. 1982.

Left: Left to right: unidentified, Naomi Kanosh, Charlie Joseph. 1984.

Above: Chilkat Dancers. 1984.

Right: Left to right: unidentified, Bessie Fred, Alice Bennett, Jennie Jim, Elizabeth Martin. 1984.

Top left: Front: Barbara Lewis. Left to right, rear: Al Porter, Maggie Adams, Maxine Thompson, James Knudson wearing Eagle hat, Thomas Bennett wearing *Deisheetaan* (Beaver) clan hat. 1982.

Above: This unidentified dancer is hiding his face to encourage people to identify him only by his crest.

Left: Left to right: unidentified, unidentified, unidentified, Sophie Marvin, Ginny Johns, J. Johns (boy), Betty Houston, Sophie Isturis Barril, Anissa Johns. 1984.

Far left: Roger Sheakley. 1984.

Left: Jerilyn George, Paul Willis wearing a Raven *Deisheetaan* (Beaver) clan hat and a Raven tunic.

Below: Left to right, front: Martha Shields holding drum, Esther Shea, Cecilia White wearing yarns, Agnes Bellinger wearing Chilkat robe, unidentified (crouching), Hazel Simeon, Joel William Corwin wearing Alaska headband, Lillian Hammond. Left to right, rear: unidentified, unidentified, Forrest DeWitt, Jr., wearing hat, unidentified (face obscured), unidentified (rear), unidentified, unidentified (man wearing Eagle headband), Kelly James wearing white ermine *shakee.át* (frontlet headdress), Ben Coronell wearing Chilkat robe and goat horn headdress, Cecilia Kunz (face partially obscured), Catrina Mitchell wearing headband, unidentified (face partially obscured), Charlie Jimmie wearing nose ring, Sam Jackson, Jr. 1984.

Opposite: Photographer Ron Klein shooting a panoramic photo in front of Centennial Hall. Klein has produced panoramic photos for every Celebration except the first one.

30 • *Celebration*

Above: Left to right, front: Nastasia Johnson, Misty Jack, Lorena Boxley, Helen Hanlon.

Above right: Left to right: Sam Sheakley wearing bear footprint shirt, Steven Adams wearing Yakutat shirt, J.P. Buller wearing blue shirt.

Right: Left to right: Dora Arlene Jack Williams, Elsie Pratt wearing a *T'akdeintaan* (Sea Pigeon) crest. 1982.

Far right: Left to right: Al Martin, Richard Dalton, *T'akdeintaan* (Sea Pigeon) clan leader. 1982.

Above: A group of young dancers wearing button blankets.

Left: Left to right: Ida Kadashan (a well-known weaver), Anna Katzeek, clan mother of the *Shangukweidí* (Thunderbird) clan. 1984.

Right: Sitka *Kaagwaantaan* (Wolf) Dancers. Left to right: Wallace Scott, Kendrick Payton (front), unidentified, Nels Lawson, Tommy Jimmie, Jr.

Honoring Our Ancestors and Cultural Survival

Above: Left to right: Dianna Druley, Cecilia Kunz, Elizabeth Martin. 1984.

Right: Left to right: Daisy Jones, Betty Goldsbury.

Haida dance group. Deanna Morrison wearing Haida headband, Cindy Frank wearing *Xaadas* (Haida) headband. 1984.

A child's perspective. Three children of the Sitka *Kaagwaantaan* (Wolf) Dancers.

Art and *At.óow*

ROSITA WORL

THE TLINGIT, HAIDA, AND TSIMSHIAN artistic tradition began several thousand years ago and through the millennia it has evolved into an art form that is distinctive in indigenous America. Art adorned everything from ceremonial objects and regalia to large and small utilitarian items and equipment and was even emblazoned on natural features throughout the homelands. So creative were the artisans that ordinary objects from bowls to canoes were extraordinary works of art. The Southeast Alaska Natives appreciated the aesthetic qualities of their masterpieces, and they accorded artisans and crafts people special status within their society. Their sacred objects and their utilitarian objects embellished with their unique art designs were appreciated foremost, however, for their spiritual and social value rather than as art objects.

The Westerners who first arrived in the homeland of the Southeast Alaska Indians immediately sought to collect both sacred and utilitarian objects made by the Tlingit, Haida, and Tsimshian. Unfortunately, as they came to understand the significance of the art objects to the Native people, they labeled them idols and the Natives who worshipped their *at.óow* heathens and pagans. This perception, however, did not stop the collecting frenzy that persisted through the 1800s and into the next century. Curio hunters were joined by museum curators and art collectors who combed Southeast Alaska looking for Native art. A few of the collectors were unscrupulous in acquiring it, even robbing grave

Opposite: **Angoon (*Teikweidí*) Brown Bear Clan hat.**

sites. Museums across the country are now filled with art collected from Southeast Alaska. One clan leader recalled the irony of the disdain of Westerners toward Native religion coupled with the relentless collection of Native art: "They collected our sins!"

As it became harder for Native peoples to maintain their traditional livelihood, which was based on subsistence hunting and fishing, they entered the cash economy. One method of acquiring cash was to produce artwork for sale to the increasing number of tourists who began to visit Alaska. Art production continued, but it was largely limited to the tourist market, which began to flourish in earnest in the late 1800s. With growing importation of pseudo-art objects made by non-Natives into the U.S., and the declining number of young artists apprenticing with master artists, which had been the traditional method of training artisans, the quality of art deteriorated. A few artists continued to produce objects for traditional and ceremonial use, but most production in the art market was for tourists. The masterpieces once produced for ceremonial uses that had brought acclaim to the Southeast Natives were mostly the creations of an earlier generation of artists. They were primarily located in museums rather than in clan houses, which had largely been abandoned by the early to mid-1900s.

At.óow

While Westerners perceive Tlingit, Haida, and Tsimshian sacred objects as art, Native people view them as "*at.óow*." The translation, "an owned or purchased object," masks their social and spiritual significance. In the Tlingit worldview, *at.óow* is multidimensional—it represents both natural and supernatural phenomena, and it has both tangible and intangible properties. *At.óow* includes the artistic design, which represents either a clan crest animal or a spiritual helper, and the physical object on which it is depicted as well as the associated names, songs, and stories. *At.óow* also embodies the spirits of both humans and supernatural entities, which met sometime in the ancient past, and the geographical site at which the event occurred.

The right to portray the visual representation of this ancient encounter was acquired by the ancestor, who generally died in the encounter as a result of an accident. His or her loss of life also conveyed to the descendants of the clan the privilege of claiming an exclusive relationship with the supernatural entity. The supernatural being is usually depicted on the *at.óow* in the form of a bird, animal, or fish, on ceremonial objects, clothing, utilitarian items and equipment, houses, canoes, totem poles, and as markers on rocks, trees, or other natural features.

Traditionally, two rituals precede creation of the *at.óow*. The first occurs when a clan formally commissions an artist to produce an object. The second is held when the commissioning clan and artist acquire the natural material to make the *at.óow*. When the artist completes the object, with its visual representation of the supernatural beings, it is then ritually presented at a larger ceremony. During the ceremonial presentation of the *at.óow*, the story of how the crest animal or spirit was acquired is recounted. Clan names are recited and songs recalling the event are sung. The host clan then kills money (formerly slaves), which is called *dáanaa dujákx* ("they kill the money") by distributing it to the guest clan.

The ritual presentation and distribution of cash and gifts by the host clan together with a response and acknowledgment by the guest clan or clans transform the object with its crest design and associated property of names, stories, songs, and the site at which the ancient encounter occurred into an *at.óow*. The recitation of names, recounting of the stories, and singing of the songs also serve to call forth the ancestors and spirits of the *at.óow*. This ceremony is repeated through the generations as the *at.óow* transfers from one guardian to the next.

This ceremony is also a legal transaction in which title to the *at.óow* is validated as the property of the host clan. The presence of the guest clan from the opposite moiety validates the host clan's ownership of the *at.óow* in the same way that a deed of title is recorded in Western or American systems. This same ritual and legal process is repeated generation after generation as succeeding clan leaders take possession of their clan's *at.óow* on behalf of their clan. The sacred significance of the *at.óow* is reaffirmed and the clan ownership is revalidated within each succeeding ceremony as the trusteeship transfers from uncle to maternal nephew.

Based on traditional Tlingit property law, all members of a clan collectively own their clan's *at.óow*. They own the intellectual property represented by the crest art, the names, stories, and songs in the same way that they hold their tangible property.

Unlike art, which is publicly displayed, *at.óow* are carefully packed away and brought out only for ceremonial rites generally referred to as k̲u.éex'. No one other than the participants in the k̲u.éex' was privileged to see clan *at.óow* in its ceremonial setting. Now, however, the public is able to see clan *at.óow* used in such secular events as the biennial Celebration. Images in this book feature some of the *at.óow* owned by clans and individuals.

At.óow in Celebration

The presence of *at.óow* in Celebration from the beginning included song and dance and regalia, including the depiction of clan crests. Occasionally clan stories and names are also recited during dance performances.

The use of *at.óow* in a public, non-ceremonial event was not taken lightly by the clan leaders and elders, who wanted to be assured that respect and reverence for the *at.óow* would be maintained and that traditional protocols would not be violated. Traditionally, clans sang and danced to their own songs and on special occasions, a child or grandchild of a clan was allowed to dance and sing with them. But Celebration spurred the formation of dance groups whose members represented multiple clans, so different clan songs were sung by the dance group. The basic rule, which was codified in all literature sent to dance groups, was that dance groups had to acknowledge clan ownership of songs they sang. The unwritten assumption was that members of clans owning the songs were also represented as members of the dance group. On occasion, clans have expressed their concern that ownership of clan songs was not acknowledged during Celebration performances.

One clan has purchased ads in the Celebration Program Guide to publish one of their songs. It cited its ownership of the song to discourage the use of this song without attributing its clan ownership.

Only two clan-based groups regularly perform in Celebration, and the regalia and songs they use are their *at.óow*. Clan *at.óow* are also used by several dance groups that represent communities such as Yakutat, Klukwan, Angoon, Haines, and Hoonah. Perhaps the most spectacular is Angoon, in which clan leaders dance in with their clan hats. The *Shangukweidí* clan is also stunning, dancing with a dozen Chilkat robes.

Almost every type of *at.óow* and regalia can be seen at Celebration, including Chilkat robes and button blankets. The interior-style Athabaskan tunics are also widely used, particularly by the Yakutat, Klukwan, and Haines dance groups that have close ties to the inland Canadian Tlingit. More recently, dance groups primarily from Washington have begun to use lightweight shawls reminiscent of the shawls used by dancers from the tribes of the lower forty-eight states. Beaded leather dresses and vests are also common. All forms of headwear are seen, from clan hats, to carved frontlets with ermine, Bear Ears, cedar and spruce root basketry hats, and all kinds of headbands. Accessories used by dancers range from beaded bibs or collars, aprons, octopus bags, leggings, moccasins, and boots. Silver bracelets and pendants with clan crests are uniformly worn by men and women during Celebration as well as throughout the year. Most all groups also have dance staffs along with their drums and rattles.

Celebration has allowed younger generations and those who are not able to attend the traditional ceremonies to see their clan *at.óow*. It has also stimulated a resurgence in regalia-making. The use of clan crests on regalia reinforces the ties between contemporary Tlingit, Haida, and Tsimshian, their ancestors, and future generations. Celebration has also assured that the voices of their ancestors will continue to be heard through the songs sung by their descendants. ■

Clan hats dance. Left to right: Double-Headed Raven hat from the Raven House in Angoon worn by Joe Bennett, Angoon L'eeneidí (Dog Salmon) hat worn by Sam Newman, Esther Littlefield (rear), Angoon Teikweidí (Brown Bear) hat worn by Eddie Jack. 1982.

Opposite: Angoon (*Teikweidí*) Brown Bear Clan hat. 1982.

Art and At.óow • 43

Early tourist masks made for sale by Willie Marks, who also was commissioned by clans to make ceremonial objects.

Above: Left to right: Paul Johnson wearing white fur headpiece (face obscured), Emma Demmert (rear), Leonard Demmert wearing *Deisheetaan* (Beaver) hat, Gilbert Fred wearing blue Octopus bag, unidentified (rear), Jessie Jim wearing red and black, Alfred Demmert wearing *Teikweidí* (Brown Bear) hat, Cindy DeWitt Paul (rear), Toni Vonda holding drum, Frank Jim wearing *Teikweidí* (Brown Bear) hat.

Top left: Tom Bennett wearing Raven *Deisheetaan* (Beaver) hat. 1982.

Left: Nels Lawson, a *Kaagwaantaan* (Wolf), wearing a *shakee.át* (frontlet headdress) and holding a Killer Whale hat.

Art and *At.óow* • 45

Left to right: Lydia George, Sam Newman wearing Angoon *L'eeneidí* (Dog Salmon) hat and Chilkat tunic, Elsie John. 1982.

Above: Left to right: Dr. Walter Soboleff, David Katzeek wearing a *Shangukweidí* (Thunderbird) Chilkat robe and Eagle hat carved by his grandfather, Dan Katzeek, a Killer Whale. 1982.

Top left: Rosita Worl, a *Shangukweidí* (Thunderbird), wearing an Eagle *shakee.át* (frontlet headdress) and Killer Whale bib. 1982.

Left: Ross Soboleff wearing Chilkat robe, Eagle necklace, and Frog headdress. 1984.

Patrick Anderson displaying a *Shangukweidí* (Thunderbird) crest on a Chilkat robe.

Art and *At.óow* • 47

Opposite: Left to right, front: Richard Austin, Cal Wilson, Jr.

Above: Left to right: Cal Wilson, Jr., unidentified, Larry Jackson holding Wolf hat, Richard Austin wearing an Eagle tunic (face partially obscured), Harriet Knudson.

Above right: Cal Wilson, Jr., wearing Wolf headdress.

Right: Left to right: Larry Jackson, Mike Jackson (rear), Richard Austin wearing Wolf hat, Harriet Knudson, Cal Wilson, Jr.

48 • Celebration

Above: Spirit dance. Left to right: Austin Hammond, George Dalton, Amos Wallace, Robert Martin, Sr. (rear), Al Widmark wearing Chilkat tunic, Richard Dalton holding Chilkat robe, Jack Strong wearing Eagle hat, Frank O. Williams (holding blanket), unidentified person wearing robe with *T'akdeintaan* (Sea Pigeon) and Octopus crests. 1982.

Above right: Left to right: Clarissa Hudson, unidentified, Al McKinley, Marlene Johnson (rear), Ann Keener, unidentified, Bessie Fred, Richard Dalton.

Right: Spirit dance. Left to right, onstage: Sam Newman wearing *L'eeneidí* (Dog Salmon) hat and Chilkat tunic, Eddie Jack wearing fur robe and Angoon *Teikweidí* (Brown Bear) Clan hat, David Willard holding peace blanket, George Jim wearing *shakee.át* (frontlet headdress), unidentified dancer wearing *gangóosh*, Cyril George (behind blanket) wearing *Deisheetaan* (Beaver) clan hat, unidentified man wearing Wolf headdress, unidentified, Larry Jackson holding blanket, William Nelson (against wall), Mary Willis wearing feather headdress, Kathryn Duncan drumming, Patti Paul (rear), Jimmie George (seated), Lydia George. 1982.

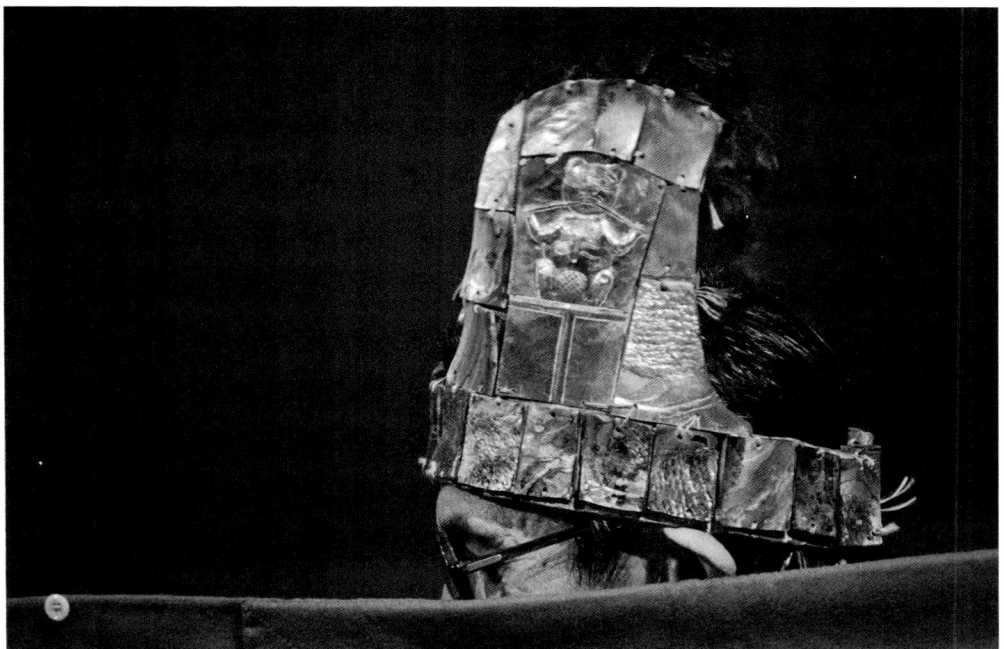

Above left: Spirit dance. Matthew Fred wearing abalone *gangóosh* with copper *Deisheetaan* (Beaver) *tináa* (coppers) inlay. 1982.

Above: Spirit dance. Angoon *L'eeneidí* (Dog Salmon) hat behind blanket, David Willard holding blanket. 1982.

Left: Spirit dance. Left to right: Joe Bennett wearing a Double-Headed Raven hat from the Raven House of Angoon, Dan Johnson holding blanket, Angoon *L'eeneidí* (Dog Salmon) hat behind blanket. 1982.

Opposite: Spirit dance. Xudzidaa Kwáan (People of Angoon) Dancers. Left to right: Victoria Johnson, Elton Willard wearing Raven's Tail blanket, unidentified, unidentified (boy in black), Seth Elisoff (child), Tamara Howard (holding blanket), Dermott Howard (behind blanket) wearing a Raven *shakee.át* (frontlet headdress), Rebekah Howard holding blanket, unidentified (rear), Patricia Mills (against backdrop), Romeo Brouillette (child), Daniel P. Brown, Sr., holding Bear staff and wearing Bear Hat and Bear Chilkat tunic, Andrew Gamble, Jr., wearing Wolf hat (rear), unidentified (child), Edwell John, Joe Hedstrom (rear), Robert Johnson.

Above: Pedro Barril wearing a carved *shakee.át* (frontlet headdress) with abalone inlays. 1982.

Left: Spirit dance. Dermott Howard with Eagle down in air as a symbol of peace.

Left to right: Irene Lampe wearing a T'akdeintaan (Sea Pigeon) crest, Sophie Marvin wearing a Bear *shakee.át* (frontlet headdress), a beaded Raven necklace and a Chilkat robe. 1982.

Art and *At.óow* • 53

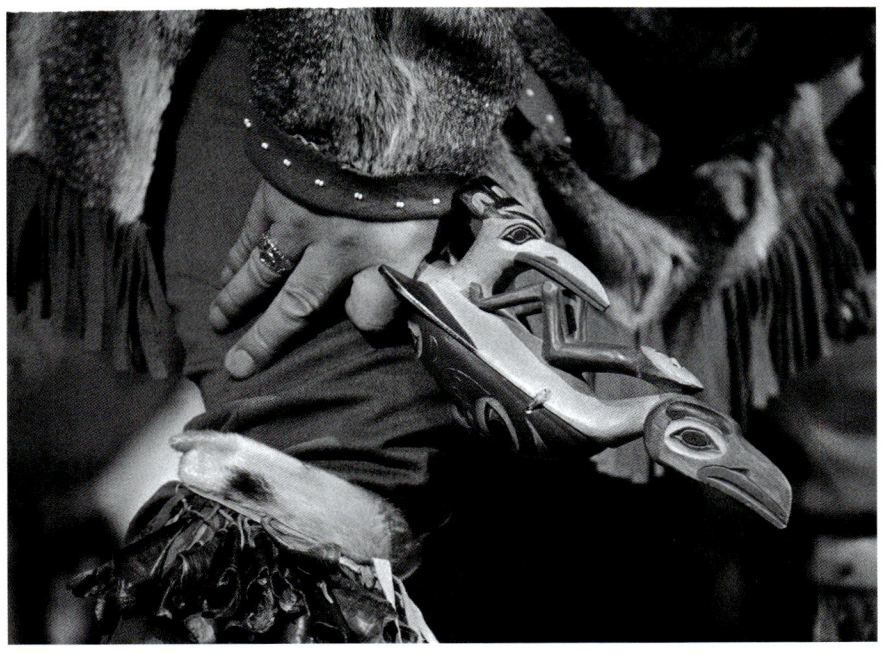

Opposite: Elizabeth Govina. A *T'akdeintaan* (Sea Pigeon) Clan robe depicting *Geesh Daax Woogoodi Yéil* (Raven Who Went Down Along the Bull Kelp).

Above: Raven rattle with Humanoid and Kingfisher and Hawk on bottom side. 1982.

Left: Eli Hanlon wearing *Wooshkeetaan* (Shark) hat. 1982.

Right: Ed Mercer wearing Killer Whale hat.

Art and *At.óow* • 55

Far left: Dorothy Coronell James, *Yanyeidí* (Eagle Wolf), holding a Wolf paddle and wearing an Eagle Wolf bib.

Above: Teslin Tlingit Dancers holding a Frog drum. Left to right: unidentified, Johnny "Taku" Jack, Charles Morris. 1982.

Left: Al McKinley displaying Eagle *Wooshkeetaan* (Shark) crests on button blanket.

Opposite, left: Raven Frog Drum.

Opposite, right: Cecelia Unick holding *Wooshkeetaan* (Shark) paddles and wearing Eagle headband and Shark tunic.

Art and At.óow • 57

Yaaw Téiyi (Herring Rock) Dancers. Left to right: Gerry Williams wearing a flowered Octopus bag, Vera Jackson (rear), Marlis Mayeda wearing *T'akdeintaan* (Sea Pigeon) crest on headband and blanket clasp, Gail Napihaa, Pietr Dabaluz (baby), Mary Ebona-Miller wearing *Deisheetaan* (Beaver) tunic, headdress and bib.

Tsimshian dancers.

G̱eisán (Marks Trail) Dancers displaying *Lukaax.ádi* (Sockeye) crests. Left to right: unidentified man wearing woven cedar hat and Chilkat robe featuring a salmon design, unidentified man wearing *gangóosh* and Chilkat robe with a whale design.

Art and *At.óow* • 59

Tlingit Ceremonial Music and Dance

Survival and Adaptation

MARIA WILLIAMS

"To resist is to retrench in the margins, retrieve what we were and remake ourselves."
—LINDA TUHIWAI SMITH[1]

How has Tlingit music changed and adapted to the twenty-first century geopolitical world? As indigenous people in Alaska come together to celebrate cultures, languages, music, and dances, we must reflect upon who we are, where we have come from, and where we are going. Over time, many adaptations have occurred as the Tlingit, Haida, and Tsimshian people have survived and continued to practice our songs and dances.

Tlingit music was inseparable from the clan-based social structure. Each clan had its own repertoire of music, dance, associated performance protocols, regalia, and styles. The Tlingit, Haida, and Tsimshian lived in clan houses, and their songs and dances were, for the most part, collectively owned. The music of the *ixt* (shaman) and the *yéik* (spirit) songs were imbued with special power and governed by separate protocols.

The Tlingit repertoire of songs included love songs, sung to guest clans during ceremonies; sorrow songs, sung during the memorial funerary ceremonies; and spirit songs, performed by the shaman and his apprentices. Special songs and dances were also associ-

Opposite: Mt. St. Elias Dancers

ated with different clan objects, such as hats. The Southeast Alaska Indians also traded for songs with their interior Athabaskan neighbors. In the 1980s, the clan leader of the *Lukaax̱.ádi* gave a song to the Tlingit, Haida, and Tsimshian which was adopted as a tribal anthem. Special songs and dances were also performed for Peace Ceremonies. During Celebration, love songs are primarily performed and occasionally spirit songs.

The revered possessions of the clan, the *at.óow,* especially the ceremonial hats, had their own songs. The hat songs were only performed during special occasions when the *at.óow* was brought out. Special protocols were meted out by the clan and house leaders. During music and dance performances, balance was maintained between the two major divisions in Tlingit society, which are referred to as moieties—the Raven and Eagle, or Crow and Wolf among the Northern Tlingit. Balance was maintained by a clan group from the Eagle side performing four songs, followed by a clan group from the Raven side performing four songs. This alternation continued throughout the night. Tlingit people also loved the music and dance of other tribes and would often invite Athabascan, Haida, Tsimshian, and even Alutiiq and Unangan dancers. But in a formal ceremonial Tlingit setting, the balance between the moieties was always maintained.

During the Russian colonial period of the late eighteenth century, music and dance remained relatively unchanged. After 1867, with the advent of the American period and the arrival of missionaries, the repression of Native languages and traditional beliefs and the loss of a substantial portion of our traditional homelands dealt a significant blow to the traditional clan-based culture, religions, and shamanism. The loss of Native languages affected music and dances.

By the 1960s, the Native people of Alaska began to work together to address their indigenous land claims. Their collective efforts led to the 1971 Alaska Native Claims Settlement Act. Music and dance became staples at every political gathering where people discussed implementation of Native land claims. By the 1980s, a cultural renaissance was born.

Celebration started during this period, in 1982. Celebration is a modern adaptation, a brilliant strategy that came about because clan leaders and elders wanted to bring the clans together to share our valued music and dance traditions. Celebration is a time for dance groups from all over southeastern Alaska and parts of Canada to gather and share.

Sometimes during Celebration, ceremonial hats and their special songs are sung and their stories told. At those moments, Celebration becomes an intersection between the ancient and the modern. Young people see revered clan possessions and hat dances that they might not ever see again, since the hats are used or brought out only at very special occasions.

As Tlingit, Haida, and Tsimshian people began to abandon their clan houses in the twentieth century, changes became evident in how clan songs and dances were brought out, how they were performed, and when they were performed. Rather than a single clan dancing and singing together, most dance groups now are combinations of individuals from different moieties and clans. Another change is the acknowledgment of clan ownership of songs. Although most songs are still owned by clans, dance groups do not uniformly identify whose clan songs they are singing, nor do they adhere to the associated traditional protocols.

The ceremonial hats and other clan-related cultural patrimony in some villages have maintained the repertoire of songs associated with them. Each clan hat for example, still has its own repertoire of songs that can only be performed when that hat is brought out. As cultural patrimony began to disappear with the collection frenzy for Northwest Coast art by museum and art collectors, these repertoires became lost because the *at.óow* was removed from the clan or village. When some of the items were returned under the Native American Graves Protection and Repatriation Act in the 1990s, the elders and clan leaders realized a significant part of their traditional repertoire of songs had been lost.

Celebration raises significant questions about the renaissance in traditional dance and music: "Do we dance and sing like we did in the 19th century? Has the cultural context changed?" Answers to these questions emphasize the work that must be accomplished to preserve and enhance Natives cultures. Clan songs that have survived must be documented. The special songs associated with the *at.óow* and clan origin or migration songs that record ceremonial histories should also be recorded. Although a relatively small number still speak our Native languages, new songs recording our ongoing clan histories should be composed. With the creation of new regalia, new songs should also be composed to accompany them, especially for the clan-based regalia.

Celebration has given us a rare opportunity to look back, but also to look forward. In essence, this is our spirit and who we are as Tlingit, Haida, and Tsimshian, who we are as indigenous people. We are the children of the survivors—those who fought for our land, our human rights, and our cultural legacy.

1. Linda Tuhiwai Smith, *Decolonizing Methodologies: Research and Indigenous Peoples* (London and New York: Zed Books, 1999), 4.

Opposite: Celebration audience. Left to right, front row: Jennie Thlunaut (wearing white headband), Katherine Mills, Elsie Pratt. Second row: Charlie Jimmie (wearing face paint), Rachael Johnson, Amy Marvin (wearing headband). Third row: Matilda Lewis, Ann Keener, Lucille Carrillo, Nellie Lord, Fred Morgan. Fourth row: unidentified (looking down), Lena Jimmie (girl with long hair, face partially obscured), Lillian Hammond, Richard King, Mary King, Cecilia Kunz. 1982.

Above: Dressing-up song. Miciana Hutcherson (wearing white) leads performers toward the stage at Centennial Hall.

Above right: Raven dance. Left to right: Austin Hammond wearing feather headdress, Johnny Marks (rear), Nathan Jackson, Jimmy Marks, Nancy Jackson dressed as Raven, Daisy Phillips (face obscured by veil), Phillip Jackson (rear), Mary Cesar (rear), Matilda Lewis (wearing black pants), Ann Keener, Gloria Sarabia (rear), Mary Paddock, Eli Phillips, Austin Hammond, Jr. (in profile). 1982.

Right: Mt. Saint Elias Dancers.

Left: 4th Generation Tsimshian Traditional Dancers. Left to right: Myranell Bergtold, unidentified.

Above: Left to right: Sam Sheakley, Gary Brown, Archie Brown III.

Tlingit Ceremonial Music and Dance • 67

Above: Mt. Saint Elias Dancers. Left to right: Brandon Johnson, Judy Ramos, J.P. Buller (rear), Maka Monture.

Above right: David James (Carl), Ellie Jackson.

Right: Left to right: John Duncan, Rachel Moreno, unidentified.

Kéex' Kwáan (People from Kake) Dancers.

Love song. Front to rear: Mamie Williams, Carol Williams, Gloria McKinley dancing for their fathers' clans.

Tlingit Ceremonial Music and Dance • 69

Left: Melvin Charles singing to children of his clan.

Above: James Knudson wearing Eagle hat. 1982.

Heinyaa Kwáan (Tribe from Across the Water). Left to right: Lisa George (front), Daniel Brown wearing white fur headdress (rear), Curtis Demmert, unidentified (boy), Teresa Kato, Emmett Fairbanks (baby), Mathew Macasaet wearing headdress (rear), Michael George wearing Raven hat, Sabrina Demmert.

Dawn Jackson, Jillian Jackson (baby).

Left to right: Fran Houston, unidentified (child), Antoinette Houston, Rosa Miller. 1984.

Young dancer from Ketchikan.

Left: Dancer wearing a Bear *shakee.át* (frontlet headdress) and small, leather Chilkat-style robe and apron. 1984.

Above: Mathew Macasaet wearing a Killer Whale Chilkat robe and *shakee.át* (frontlet headdress).

Tlingit Ceremonial Music and Dance • 73

Above: Left to right: Elsie John, Eddie Jack (front) wearing Angoon *Teikweidí* (Brown Bear) clan hat, Gerald Gamble (rear) wearing *Deisheetaan* (Beaver) *shakee.át* (frontlet headdress) and Double-Headed Raven tunic, Al Zuboff wearing Raven headdress and tunic. 1982.

Above right: Teslin Tlingit Dancers. 1982.

Right: Frank Coronell.

Above left: Left to right, rear: Viola Burgess, Esther Nix, Cindy Frank, Grace DeWitt, Deanna Morrison (wearing Haida headband). Front: Don Sanderson, unidentified, unidentified. 1982.

Above: Left to right: Dionne Jackson holding Frog drum, Louise Brady holding a Killer Whale drum.

Left: Left to right, front: Elton Willard, Owen James, Ernest Jack.

Above: Danny Jackson with Killer Whale hat and staff, wearing Octopus and Killer Whale tunic.

Above right: Healing ceremony. Charlie Jimmie dancing with feathers and a Raven rattle. Left to right, rear: Nora Dauenhauer (against wall), Rosita Worl wearing Chilkat robe, Nathan Jackson, Lillian Hammond, Matilda Lewis, Ann Keener, Mary Paddock, Eli Phillips. On floor: Austin Hammond, Jr.. 1982.

Right: Left to right, front: Joe Thomas holding Killer Whale staff, Wilfred Skeek wearing beaded headdress, tunic and Eagle leggings.

Left: Interior-style clothing and dance with snow shoes. Left to right, front: Austin Hammond wearing Raven crest on leather tunic, Nathan Jackson wearing a leather Chilkat-style apron and Chilkat leggings, Phillip Jackson, Eli Phillips. 1982.

Below: Mt. St. Elias Dancers. Front: J.P. Buller wearing tunic with Beaver and Wolf crests.

Far left: Left to right: unidentified man wearing *Wooshkeetaan* (Shark) headdress, Marlene Johnson, Irene Lampe. 1982.

Left: Myrna Chaney.

Lower left: Esther Littlefield singing to clan children, wearing Raven headdress and beaded, Octopus bag. 1982.

Left: A small drummer wearing a button blanket.

Above: Lillian Hillman singing to clan children.

A small drummer from Hoonah wearing a button blanket. Rear: Johanna Church.

Xaadas Git'aláng (Children of the Haida) Dancers. Front: Richard Rinehart leads young Lejon Robertson, Jr., a Haida Eagle, followed by Kenneth Morris, a Haida Eagle.

Matthew Fred. 1982.

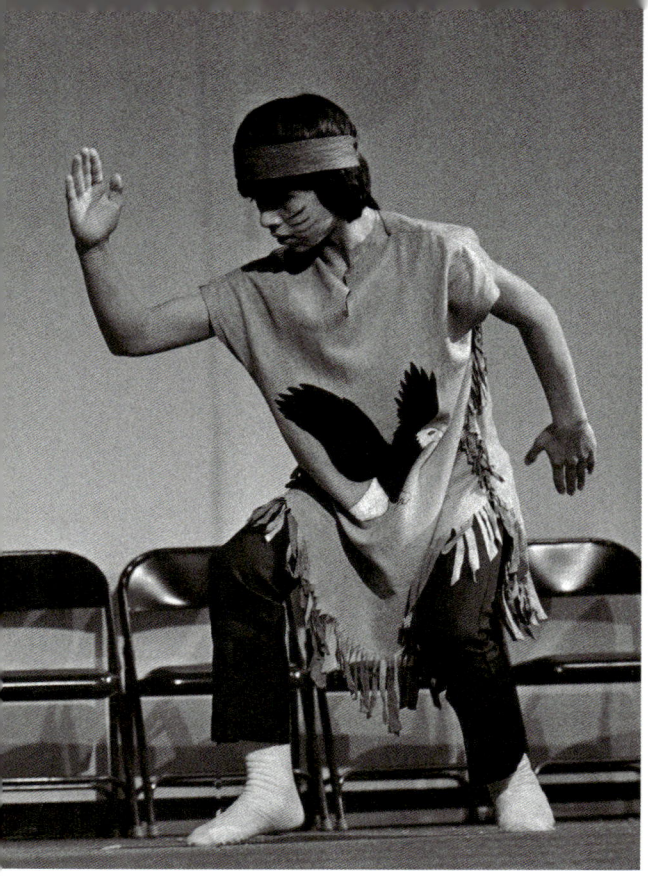

Above: Don Sanderson.

Above right: Left to right: Teresa Moses, Heather Powell singing a love song.

Right: Tommy Jimmie, Jr. 1982.

Far right: Timothy Lindoff holding Eaglehead staff and wearing a Wolf apron and headband.

82 • *Celebration*

Above left: Left to right, rear: Ethel Makinen, Alice Williams, Vida Davis. Front: Bernice James, Annie Joseph, Mary Marks, Mary Perkins, Esther Littlefield.

Above: All Nation's Children Dancers. Left to right: Miciana Hutchenson, Ruby Soboleff, Katie Wade.

Left: All Nation's Children Dancers. Left to right: Galen Wright, Leandrea Makaily, Raven Joey, Julie Lanz, Joni Skrzynski.

Above: Left to right: Al McKinley, Herb Sheakley, Amelia Lafferty.

Above right: Peace ceremony. George Dalton, *Kaagwaantaan* (Wolf), representing the Deer, a symbol of peace, flanked by *T'akdeintaan* (Sea Pigeon) clan members, left to right: Eddie Sarabia, Richard Dalton (rear), Frank O. Williams. 1982.

Right: Daaxaat Kanadaa (Water Flows All Around Kootznahoo Inlet) Dancers. Left to right: Joe Hedstrom (rear), unidentified, Norman Vonda wearing Raven *shakee.át* (frontlet headdress), Lori Dugdale (rear), William Bennett wearing Raven's Tail robe, George Jim, Jr., wearing Chilkat robe and Raven *shakee.át* (frontlet headdress), Edwell John wearing *Dakl'aweidí* (Killer Whale) clan hat, Paul Bennett holding staff. The Eagle down in the air represents peace.

Far left: Paul Bennett holding Brown Bear staff.

Above: Daaxaat Kanadaa (Water Flows All Around Kootznahoo Inlet) Dancers. Left to right: Lori Dugdale wearing *Deisheetaan* (Beaver) design, Patricia Mills (rear), Carolee Martin, *Deisheetaan* (Beaver), Romeo Brouillette (boy), Darren Austin, singing to children of their clan.

Left: Viola Burgess. 1982.

Tlingit Ceremonial Music and Dance • 85

Opposite page:

Top left: A woman and child dancing in support of veterans.

Top right: Norman Williams shakes hands with Ralph Knudson.

Bottom: Recognition of veterans. Left to right: Helen Hanlon, Paul Willis, Marcelo Quinto, William Kanosh, George Paul, Charles Williams, Gerald Bennett, Joe Bennett holding staff, unidentified.

Above: Left to right: Misty Jack, Alice Haldane, Amber Lampe, unidentified.

Right: Left to right: Austin Hammond (back to camera), Agnes Bellinger, Nathan Jackson (rear), Jimmy Marks wearing *shakee.át* (frontlet headdress), Charlie Jimmie, Doug Patterson holding *tináa* (coppers), Ann Keener, unidentified. 1982.

86 • *Celebration*

Richard Dalton wearing tunic with Frog Salmon crest. 1982.

88 • *Celebration*

Left to right: Ashley Johnston, Leroy Peratrovich, Nicole George.

Craig Island Dancers. Front to rear: Jeff Sheakley, Jr., Bear Yates (holding feathers), Sam Sheakley, Kerri Sheakley, A.J. Wilson (child), Drew Handley (child), (?) Peratrovich, Kristen Sheakley, unidentified, unidentified.

Above: Craig Island Dancers. Left to right, front: Jacob (?), (?) Anderson, Emmitt Benolken.

Above right: Paul Johnson.

Right: Left to right: Donelle Raelynn Coronell, Eunice James Lee (rear), Teesha Jodeen Wilson, Charles M. Brouillette (front), unidentified (rear), Janice See, Diane Macasaet.

A group of young dancers performs at the Alaska Native Brotherhood Hall, one of several performance venues at Celebration.

Left to right: unidentified, Krista Bontrager (rear), Galen Wright wearing black and blue button blanket, Torianna Fogg (front), unidentified (rear), Antonia Fogg, LaDonna Rinehart (rear, wearing hat), Danelle Kasnick. The blue and red hats with dangling beads were adapted from sailor hats.

Above: 4th Generation Tsimshian Traditional Dancers. Left to right: Jennifer McCarty, Glenn Guthrie, Vincent Dundas, Sr.

Left: Roger Sheakley, Jessie Gray. 1984.

Right: A dancer displaying a carved moon.

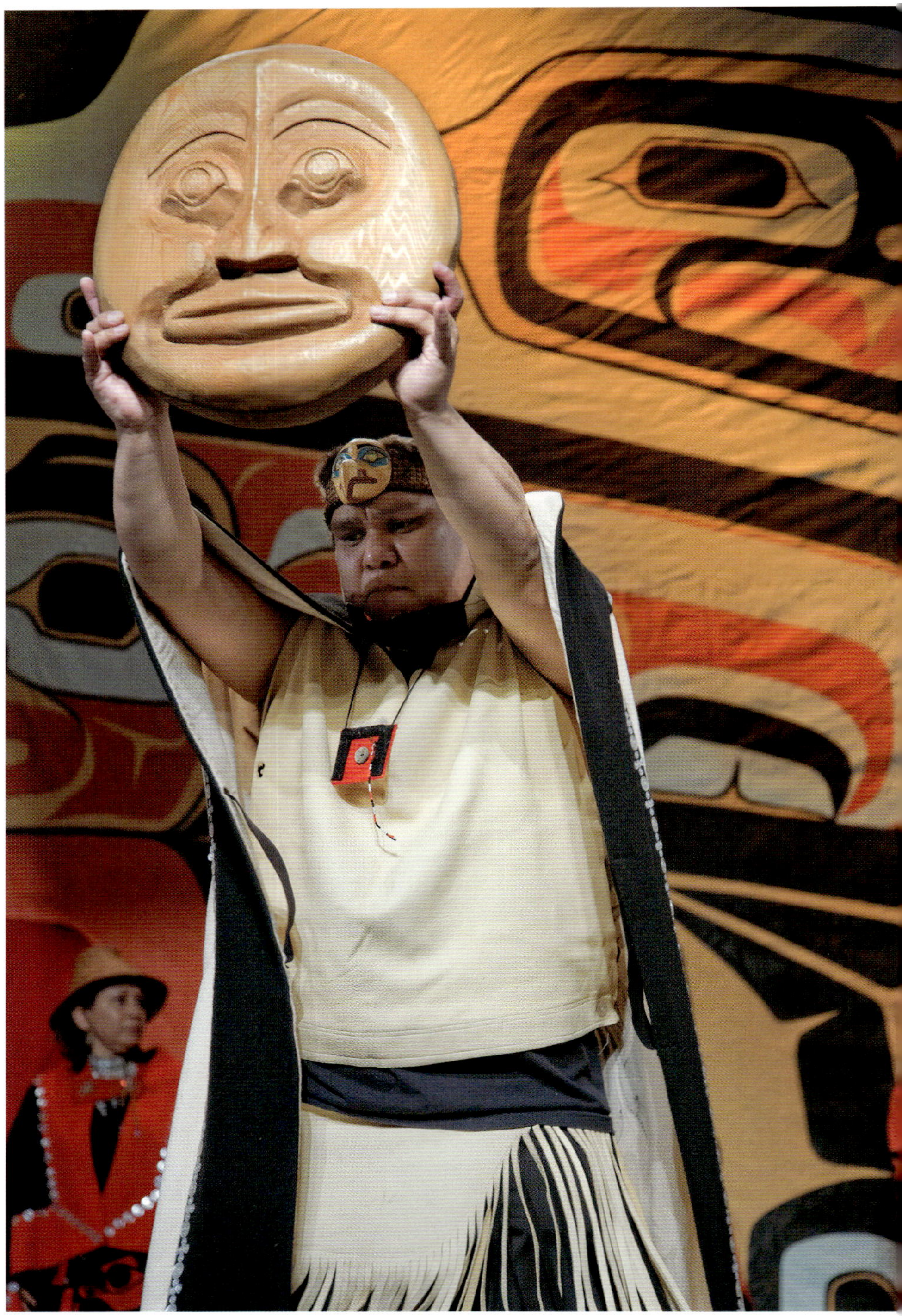

Left: Dancers from Kake.

Lower right: K̲éex̲' Kwáan (People from Kake) Dancers. Left to right: Ruth Demmert, Ellie Jackson.

Lower left: Martha Shields speaking during Celebration. 1984.

Tlingit Ceremonial Music and Dance • 93

Opposite: Heinyaa Kwáan (Tribe from Across the Water). Left to right: Jon Rowan holding staff, Patti Rowan, Eva Rowan, Mathew Macasaet wearing *shakee.át* (frontlet headdress), Jack Brown (rear), unidentified, unidentified.

Above: Yaaw Téiyi (Herring Rock) Dancers. Left to right: Marti Corpuz, Marrisa Corpuz (back to camera), Jackie Johnson, president, National Congress of American Indians, Kristen (?) (rear), Vicki Soboleff (front), unidentified, unidentified, Kerri Sheakley holding A.J. Wilson.

Right: Naa Luudisk Gwaii Yátx'i (Children of the Islands Who Learn). Traditionally, woven hats with dangling copper were placed on girls to teach them to walk with grace. If a girl was not walking properly, the coppers dangled.

Above left: Yaaw Téiyi (Herring Rock) Dancers. Left to right: Marti Corpuz (holding dance paddle), Deedee Ebona (rear, wearing red tunic), Mike Corpuz (wearing purple robe), Amy Michel (front, center), Sharon Harris (rear, wearing Eagle headband), Cameron Sheakley (child), Kerri Sheakley holding baby A.J. Wilson, Mary Ebona-Miller (holding paddle).

Above: Front to rear, left to right: Nancy Barnes, Marcella Foster, unidentified (child), Lisa Gray, Brandy Hinchman (child), MarTina Dundas, last four individuals unidentified.

Left: A dancer making an impression on a child.

Right: Love song. Left to right, front: Jacob Pratt, III, Mary Wilson, Mary Johnson, Veronica Dalton singing to children of their clan. 1984

Below: Center: Aaron Brown.

Catrina Mitchell wearing a Raven blanket clasp and dress. 1984.

Opposite: Left to right, Geraldine Ann Gray, Lillian Hillman, Veronica Dalton, Sharon Grant.

Above: Shungukweidí (Thunderbird) Clan and children and grandchildren of the *Shungukweidí*.

Left: Left to right, unidentified, George Jim, Jr., William Bennett, Bryon Jack, Jr., Denise Bennett holding Jordan Kelly Bennett, unidentified.

Tlingit Ceremonial Music and Dance • 99

Ceremonial Masks of the Tlingit, Haida, and Tsimshian

ROSITA WORL

MASKS ARE USED by the Tlingit, Haida, and Tsimshian for ceremonial purposes and in the present day, they are also used in secular events such as the Sealaska Heritage Institute Celebration and in theatrical performances. The use of ceremonial masks and the ideological systems which gave rise to it nearly succumbed to Western religions, which discouraged Native belief systems and traditional practices.

Since the late 1960s and the early 1970s, Native people began to bring their traditional practices into the open and allowed non-Natives to witness their ancient dances and traditions, including the use of masks. They also began to re-introduce ceremonies that had lain dormant for decades. Robert Davidson, an internationally acclaimed Haida artist, describes the reintroduction of the "welcoming ceremony for the salmon." In this ceremony, a dancer using a very large mask depicts the Spirit of the Salmon who dances "as a salmon with a new song, giving thanks for its return."

Masks served three functions among the Tlingit, Haida, and Tsimshian: transformation of an individual into a supernatural being; clan dramatization; and conflict resolution. With the use of masks, individuals could transform themselves into the spirit depicted by the mask. In clan dramatization or theatrical performances, dancers re-enacted clan legends. In the past, ridicule masks were also used to resolve conflicts.

Opposite: Git-Hoan (People of the Salmon) Dancers. Killer Whale mask.

Transformation Masks

Transformation masks allowed individuals who donned the mask, usually within the context of a ritual or ceremonial setting, to become symbolically transformed into a supernatural being. Transformation masks and frontlet headdresses continue to be used by lay persons in spirit dances. In this ceremony, two individuals hold a blanket in front of a dancer and only the mask and frontlet are visible above it. The dancer imitates the movement of the animal spirit depicted by the mask or frontlet. This dance is also performed at Celebration, more often by the Angoon dancers who are viewed as one of the more traditional groups.

Shamans had up to eight masks that were representations of their spirits. They acquired their spirits from their predecessor or through their own spiritual quest. The shaman used his mask during healing rituals as well as in ceremonial activities. Through the use of his mask, he was able to call on the spirits to heal the sick or ailing person, to bring good fortune, and to assist in war. The shaman was transformed into the spirit represented by the mask and became his agent.

Masks were transferred through succeeding generations to individuals who had apprenticed to their clan's shaman and had been selected by the spirit to become the next shaman. In some instances, individuals did not seek or wish to become shamans, but they were chosen by a spirit to do so. Shamans would have masks carved of their newly acquired spirit.

While shamanism has all but disappeared, ideologies surrounding shamans' objects persist. Many Natives continue to believe that masks embody spirits, and a shaman's mask can be handled only by his clan members, since the spirit embodied in the mask might harm a non-clan member who touches it.

The Southeast Alaska Indians placed great importance on the face, and the faces depicted by the masks are metaphors in oratory that represent the entire clan or tribe at a ceremony or public event. Masks of human faces also represent clan ancestors.

Clan Dramatization

Masks continue to be used to commemorate the origin and other significant events of the history of clans. They are used in ceremonial contexts with singers and dancers re-enacting the event and with clan leaders recounting the oral traditions associated with the masks. At this time, the dancer wearing the mask enters the domain of the sacred. During other ceremonies, clan masks are prominently displayed for guests to view.

The large clan houses and the architectural design with tiered floors encircling the bottom floor was a perfect setting for clan dramatization performances. Additionally, natural theaters formed in the landscapes near villages were also favorites for performances. One such natural amphitheater is on the hillside above the Chilkoot River in the Haines area, where the Tlingit congregated to watch theatrical performances enacting clan histories and legends.

In the contemporary period, Tlingit, Haida, and Tsimshian masks are used in theatrical performances. The Sealaska *Naa Kahidi* (Clan House) and other theater groups regularly used masks in their plays, which are based on oral traditions of the Tlingit, Haida, and Tsimshian. Many Native people continue to believe that they have a special relationship to the spirit depicted by the mask.

Conflict Resolution

The Southeast Alaska Indians had several mechanisms for resolving conflicts. One for resolving lesser offenses is the use of "ridicule masks" to exert social pressure on individuals who had offended members of another clan. The placement of a human mask in a public location signified that a clan was offended by the action of another clan. The mask was removed only after restitution had been made and the conflict was resolved.

One of the best known ridicule masks is of "Lying Woman." It was made of a woman who constantly gossiped about her husband. Her husband's clan was offended by her transgressions and commissioned a mask of the wife. After she had been punished by her clan and restitution made to her husband's clan, the mask was removed from public display.

Transformation and clan dramatization masks continue to be used by the Southeast Alaska Indians in ceremonial and secular events, but the use of conflict resolution masks has largely disappeared. During Celebration, the favorite dance group performances are those which use the gigantic clan dramatization masks. Notable dance groups include a Haida group led by Robert Davidson and a Tsimshian group headed by David Boxley, Sr. Davidson and Boxley are acclaimed Northwest Coast artists, and Celebration provides an opportunity to see the clan dramatization masks come to life in live performances.

Opposite: Git-Hoan **(People of the Salmon) Dancers. David Brendible wearing Raven mask.**

106 • *Celebration*

Opposite left: Git-Hoan (People of the Salmon) Dancers. Wayne Hewson wearing Killer Whale Mask.

Opposite right: Haida mask with a Shark or a Dog Fish spirit. 1982.

Below: Git-Hoan (People of the Salmon) Dancers. David Boxley wearing Eagle Transformation mask.

Right: Git-Hoan (People of the Salmon) Dancers. David Boxley preparing to open Eagle Transformation mask.

Lower right: Git-Hoan (People of the Salmon) Dancers. David Boxley with Eagle Transformation mask transformed.

Above: Git-Hoan (People of the Salmon) Dancers. Cindy James wearing Eagle mask.

Top right: Spirit dance by a Haida group. Left to right: William Wallace, unidentified, Marion Hawkins (rear), Cindy Frank (holding blanket), dancer wearing Human mask, Deanna Morrison (holding blanket), Lorena John. 1982.

Right: Spirit dance. Left to right: Peggy Akagi, Joe Zuboff wearing Sleeping Man Mask, Sharon Zuboff.

Above: Dancer wearing a Raven maskette.

Top center: A Raven mask by Reg Davidson and Raven's Tail blanket by Marie Oldfield backstage awaiting the *Tuul G̲undlaas Xyaal Xaadee* (Rainbow Creek) Dancers.

Top right: Tuul G̲undlaas Xyaal Xaadee (Rainbow Creek) Dancers. A dancer performing a Raven dance. The dance illustrates the chatty Raven, and the beak moves frequently during the performance.

Right: Tuul G̲undlaas Xyaal Xaadee (Rainbow Creek) Dancers. Raven Discovering the Light dance. Performer Terri-Lynn Williams-Davidson wearing a Moon mask by Ben Davidson, dancer wearing a Raven mask by Reg Davidson.

Above: Dancer wearing Eagle maskette with abalone inlays and otter pelts. 1982.

Right: Curtis Demmert wearing a Human maskette.

Left and below: Tuul Gundlaas Xyaal Xaadee (Rainbow Creek) Dancers. Frog mask. *Jing* (Robert Long) doing a Frog dance.

Right: Tuul Gundlaas Xyaal Xaadee (Rainbow Creek) Dancers. Frog mask. Jay Baker doing a Frog dance.

Ceremonial Masks of the Tlingit, Haida, and Tsimshian • 111

Above: **Tuul Gundlaas Xyaal Xaadee** (Rainbow Creek) Dancers. Peggy Shannon holding Shark masks by Duane Pasco (left) and Robert Davidson.

Above and right: **Tuul Gundlaas Xyaal Xaadee** (Rainbow Creek) Dancers. Dancer doing a Shark dance, wearing a Shark mask by Robert Davidson, whose father is of the Haida Shark clan, a sub-clan of the Raven clan.

Above left: Tuul Gundlaas Xyaal Xaadee (Rainbow Creek) Dancers. Left to right: Robert Davidson, *Jing* (Robert Long) doing a prelude to the Eagle transformation.

Above: Tuul Gundlaas Xyaal Xaadee (Rainbow Creek) Dancers. Eagle transformed.

Left: Tuul Gundlaas Xyaal Xaadee (Rainbow Creek) Dancers. Reg Davidson doing a *Gagiid* (Wild Man) dance, wearing a mask by Robert Davidson. This performance illustrates what may happen to a person who goes into hypothermia after his canoe capsizes. He survives, but the hypothermia makes him a bit crazy, and he transforms into a wild man with long hair and superhuman powers who lives the rest of his life in the forest. Robert Davidson's grandfather once told him, "It's a person whose spirit is too strong to die."

Becoming the Mask

ROBERT DAVIDSON

Masks play important roles in many ceremonies, displaying one's crests, illustrating myth, personal, and clan histories, calling on the supernatural and spirit beings, and transforming one into another. Our words for masks can give us insight into their roles. For example, the Haida word for mask is *niijangu,* which means "to imitate." When the mask is danced accompanied by the song, the dancer becomes the mask. This is true magic in which three are becoming one.

I have witnessed many dances from the last generation, and two occasions stand out for me. In the first, my grandmother was in her eighties as she put on a mask and we sang "I'm in awe" song. She was one with the song, mask, and dance. The other dance was when an elder gentleman from Angoon at Celebration many years ago danced the Beaver Dance behind a blanket. During the dance, all you could see was the top of the beautifully carved Beaver helmet as if it was swimming in the water. The dancer went back and forth behind the blanket and at a certain point you could hear the Beaver slapping its tail, just as if you were on the lake where the Beaver lived. At the sound of the tail slapping, the Beaver dived down behind the blanket. After a few beats of the song, the Beaver reappeared. This cycle happened a few times during the song. For both these dances, the dancer became the mask, and the audience was held captive until the dance ended.

Transformation masks illustrated the transformation of Raven into Human, Killer Whale into Human, Eagle into itself, and so on. One aspect of transformation is to demonstrate the ability to achieve cleanliness of mind and body through fasting and drinking salt water for several days. This renders the faster transparent, and when transparency is achieved, we touch the realm of supernatural. When we enter into the supernatural world of Killer Whale, being in the water is just like being in the air. We see Killer Whales in their house as human beings and very close by the door are their Killer Whale cloaks. Upon entering back into our world, we see Killer Whales wearing their cloaks.

Spirit or portrait masks help us to connect with our spirituality. In memorials, these masks bring back a deceased loved one or one held in high esteem into our world one more time so that we can clear the air and complete our time with this person.

There is a thin thread connecting us to our ancestors. We almost lost the magic and meaning of the mask, the Being One with the masked dancer to create awe and wonder and transform into Myth Time. We are on the threshold of a new journey and it is our challenge, right, and responsibility to make it meaningful.

It is a privilege and honor for the artists, singers, and dancers to illustrate and display our journey, whether by telling a story, bringing into our realm the supernatural beings, or claiming ownership to crests through these masks. Each clan has its own combination of crests which identifies their place in the world, and some masks validate their right of ownership and use of crests in public gatherings.

We have come full circle with the re-emergence of the artists. We have many artists creating masks, and many dancers and singers singing the songs of the ancient ones. We have reconnected the broken link that separated us from the ancient wisdom that fed our being, our minds, and our spirituality that has been empty for generations.

The mask imitates the being. The dancer makes the mask real. The song connects us all with our spirit. We can now become the mask.

Above: *Git-Hoan* (People of the Salmon) Dancers. David Brendible wearing Raven mask.

Right: *Git-Hoan* (People of the Salmon) Dancers. David R. Boxley wearing Mosquito mask.

Opposite: *Git-Hoan* (People of the Salmon) Dancers. Left to right: Jeff Jainga, Nick James wearing Killer Whale mask, Cindy James.

Ceremonial Masks of the Tlingit, Haida, and Tsimshian • 117

Above: Git-Hoan (People of the Salmon) Dancers. Left to right: Lloyd Brown, Cindy James, Nick James wearing Killer Whale mask, David Brendible wearing Raven headdress (rear), Tristen James

Above right: Left to right: David Willard, Wolf mask, Larry Jackson, holding blanket. 1982.

Right: Randy Gamble wearing Wolf mask.

Above left: Git-Hoan (People of the Salmon) Dancers. David R. Boxley wearing Shaman Mask, Cindy James on floor.

Above: Git-Hoan (People of the Salmon) Dancers. Wayne Hewson wearing a *Nax Nox* style mask used in a dance called the Spirit of the Potlatch.

Left: Tuul G̲undlaas Xyaal Xaadee (Rainbow Creek) Dancers. Reg Davidson playing Mercedes, a big flirt who arrives to give comic relief.

Celebration Events

ROSITA WORL

THE INAUGURAL CELEBRATION began in 1982 with 200 dancers. It was primarily a dance festival. An ancillary event was held with clan leaders, lawyers, and anthropologists who met to delineate the principles of Tlingit property law. Since then, Celebration has grown to include over forty dance groups with nearly 2,000 dancers, half of them young people who were almost invisible in the first Celebration. Additionally, Celebration now includes several major events devoted to the celebration and study of different elements of Tlingit, Haida, and Tsimshian cultures.

Parade

Celebration begins with a Grand Entrance in which all dance groups dance into the Centennial Hall in Juneau. They are led by a dance group which had been previously selected by the Sealaska Heritage Institute Board of Trustees. The Grand Entrance is a joyous occasion, with parents and grandparents proudly dancing with their children and grandchildren. Some dancers are wearing their new regalia or clan regalia that had been passed down through the generations. They have prepared for this day by learning new songs or practicing old ones. Family members and friends are busy taking pictures of their kin to

Opposite: Canoe racers in Gastineau Channel, Juneau. Left to right, SEARHC team led by captain Doloresa Cadiente, One People team led by captain Michael Chilton, Renegades team led by captain William Brown.

preserve the moment. Throughout the next three days, individual dance groups will perform in a packed hall that seats approximately 1,000. More often every seat is taken, but seats in the front are reserved for elders. When they arrive, they are escorted to their seats. Although Celebration is open to the public, the limited seating in Centennial Hall means that relatively few non-Natives are able to attend.

As Celebration continued to grow, the organizers decided to host a parade through town. Rain or shine, the parade begins at the southern end of town and nearly 2,000 follow the lead dance group through the narrow streets of Juneau. The elders who are not able to dance the mile or more are seated on an open truck bed. Even if it rains, the guest Hawaiian or Maori dance group dances in their own regalia, which is best suited for tropical weather. On occasion, dance groups stop and perform before they are prodded on by the parade marshals. The dancers stop momentarily at the Sealaska Plaza to hear guest speakers, but the palpitating energy and enthusiasm of the young dancers doesn't accommodate long speeches, and they move on toward Centennial Hall. Spectators applaud the dancers. Celebration is held during the first week in June and the population of Juneau can increase by 10,000 in a single day as tourists come off the cruise ships to witness it.

The parade is also an opportunity for the entire community, visitors, and tourists to see traditional dancing and magnificent ceremonial regalia and objects they might not otherwise see in motion. For the dancers, it is an opportunity to dance in unity with their Tlingit, Haida, and Tsimshian brothers and sisters. The parade is a visible sign of the survival and strength of Southeast Alaska Native culture.

Native Artist Market

Nowadays, Native artists produce art for both public sale and for ceremonial and tribal use. The Sealaska Heritage Institute supports Native artists through its sponsorship of a market during Celebration and at other larger events such as the annual Juneau Gallery Walk. Additionally, Native artists also sell their work through SHI's website.

The Native Artist Market was established to support the perpetuation of Southeast Alaska Native art with the quality and aesthetic forms that gave rise to its distinction and to create a broader market for Southeast Alaska Native artists. The art market and tourist shops are increasingly flooded with fake art mass-produced in foreign countries. One of the market's critical goals is protecting the authenticity of Southeast Alaska Native Arts by Native artisans. Thus the market is limited to artists who are members of federally recognized tribes and meet the requirement of the Indian Arts and Crafts Act of 1990 (PL 101-644). Additionally, Tlingit, Haida, and Tsimshian who are Canadian citizens are allowed to participate. These requirements assure consumers that the items they purchase are made by an Indian artisan and/or an Indian tribe. Although open to eligible artists, the market is generally limited to forty Native artists because of space constraints.

Artists are also required to comply with Southeast Alaska Native traditional laws. They must respect clan ownership of crests, names, songs, and other such cultural and intellectual property of clans and use only designs that are not owned by other clans in their artwork.

The arts and crafts sold at the Native Artist Market range from traditional regalia to contemporary Northwest Coast clothing. Northwest jewelry, masks, drums, dolls, and decorative arts can be purchased at the market. Sea otter, seal, deer, and moose skin products are also sold, as are buttons, beads, and carving tools.

Juried Art Show and Competition

The first Sealaska Juried Art Show and Competition began in 2002 with the objective of showcasing contemporary Southeast Alaska Native art and artisans as well as art of Tlingit, Haida, and Tsimshian living in Canada. Although Tlingit, Haida, and Tsimshian art is classified as part of the Northwest Coast art tradition, the organizers elected to limit the show to artists of Tlingit, Haida, and Tsimshian heritage. The show was also implemented to encourage and enhance the production of Native objects of artistic and commercial value which had fallen into disuse and were becoming rare. Another goal was to encourage and recognize the best possible artistic work among the Native artisans.

The final stated goal, which immediately proved controversial, was to encourage development of new forms of art based on the Northwest Coast art traditional formline and design. However, Northwest Coast art which was viewed as contemporary was not included in the first show. Contemporary Native artists expressed concern that a bias existed towards "traditional" Northwest Coast art, and a separate category for "contemporary art" was included in the second show.

The Sealaska Heritage Institute had been warned that Native artists would not participate in a juried art show, based on experiences at the Alaska State Museum. To encourage participation, Sealaska offered prizes totaling over $10,000. It proved to be a learning experience for both Sealaska and Native artists, but the show attracted nearly two dozen artists.

The First Juried Art Show and Competition received immediate recognition when internationally-acclaimed Haida artist Robert Davidson agreed to serve as the head juror. He was assisted by Aldona Jonaitis, a widely known Northwest Coast art scholar who has published numerous books and curated national exhibitions on Northwest Coast art. Both Davidson and Jonaitis guided the development of the show.

The show has outgrown its space in the Sealaska Plaza Lobby, and its success has been demonstrated by an increasing number of artists and the range and quality of art exhibited. Numerous pieces have been sold to museums and collectors throughout the state and country.

Tsimshian artist David Boxley, who won first and second place in the traditional category in 2006, reflected after receiving his award that, "Northwest Coast art, especially the art from the Tsimshian, Tlingit, and Haida, surpasses so many of the so-called ancient cultures . . . and it is still at a high level and increasing all the time which is a good thing for all artists!" His first place piece, *"Fooled You Again" Raven Transformation Mask,* was purchased by Sealaska Corporation for its collection and is currently exhibited in the Sealaska Plaza Lobby.

Language and Cultural Workshops

Building on the direction set by clan leaders and elders, the Sealaska Heritage Institute Board of Trustees in 1997 adopted Native language preservation and restoration as its foremost priority and immediately set about implementing language programs and activities. One of the quickest ways to reach a broad audience was through Celebration. The newly formed Language Department organized a series of educational Tlingit, Haida, and Tsimshian language workshops that are now a regular feature of Celebration.

In honor of the new millennium, Celebration 2000 included new activities, including the publication of *Celebration 2000: Restoring Balance Through Culture,* a collection of writings by traditional and academic scholars. Celebration 2000 was further commemorated by *The Blanket of Knowledge* which portrays a Chilkat robe designed by the institute and made by Pendleton. Leaders of the last century were also honored at Celebration 2000.

Celebration now regularly includes workshops on Northwest Coast art following the Juried Art Show and Competition awards. Guest speakers have included such notables as Bill Holm, who is best known for his analysis of Northwest Coast art, and artists such as Robert Davidson and Preston Singletary.

Workshops on the Southeast Alaska Indian cultures and historical events are also regularly held. In the past, the Native American Graves Protection and Repatriation Act of 1990, the Alaska Native Claims Settlement Act of 1971, and shamanism have been discussed. The general practice is to include both traditional scholars and academics who specialize in Tlingit, Haida, and Tsimshian studies as presenters.

Black Seaweed Contest

The Celebration Black Seaweed Contest began as a dispute among the members of the Board of Trustees of the Sealaska Heritage Institute over which seaweed tasted best. The trustees decided to hold its first seaweed contest with independent judges in Celebration

2002. The trustees were also concerned that some traditional methods of preparing seaweed were being lost.

One of the favorite types of seaweed eaten by Southeast Alaska Indians is black seaweed—*laak'ásk*. Seaweed is rich in minerals and vitamins and has been a valuable food source for the Native people of Southeast Alaska for thousands of years. Fresh seaweed grows in dark green sheets and is gathered in summer at low tide. Some people dry it in the sun while others use modern appliances. The pieces are combined with flavorings such as clam juice, minced clams, sugar, and salt. When the seaweed is almost dried, it is put through a grinder. Seaweed can be cooked with other foods or eaten dried (a form of seaweed known to Southeast Alaska Natives as "Indian popcorn").

Seaweed Names					
TLINGIT	TSIMSHIAN	HAIDA	SCIENTIFIC	ENGLISH	JAPANESE
Laak'ásk	hla-ashg	Sgíw	*Porphyra*	laver	Nori

The names of the judges remain confidential until Celebration. Judges taste the seaweed in a blind tasting, so the panel does not know the identities or hometowns of contestants. Judges assess the entries based on personal preferences. Some judges give points for seaweed prepared with no added ingredients while others prefer the sea vegetable prepared with clam juice and other enhancers. The grand prize for the Seaweed King or Seaweed Queen is $500, second prize is $250, and third prize, $100. Past winners included two sisters from Kake and a mother and son from Angoon.

"I like it natural, a little salty, and not too crunchy," said Joe Bennett, Jr., a Juneau resident who was raised in Angoon and who served as a judge. "Growing up in the village, it's part of our food and our culture and you get used to the taste."

Julie Coburn of Kasaan, who has also served as a judge, said she dries seaweed on top of the refrigerator if the weather isn't cooperating. Other people use a microwave, but Coburn doesn't think it tastes as good that way. You can also use a regular oven on low, but you have to take care that it doesn't burn, she said. Other judges said they've known people to dry seaweed under a sun lamp, or even put it in a cloth bag and throw it in a clothes dryer.

Black seaweed lovers talk about seemingly endless ways to use it—in chop suey and stir-fried dishes, with salmon eggs or herring eggs, in stews and fish-head soup, with hamburger and pork chops, with sautéed onions, or mixed with seal oil and minced clams.

"I like it ground into smaller chunks and I like it less salty," said Ted Auker, who served as a judge. He recalled eating it frequently as a child. "We call it Indian popcorn, but if you eat too much of it, it expands. That's why our babies have big chubby cheeks," he said, laughing.

Canoe Races

The Northwest Coast tribes from the coastal region of the Washington and Oregon border northward to Yakutat had fairly similar cultural characteristics that are evident through their art, architecture, and ceremonies, which are generally referred to as "potlatches." These similarities were in part due to the continuous trading and social contacts among the tribes. The maritime routes provided easy access between the communities and travel was greatly enhanced by large cedar canoes. Haida canoes, which could measure up to fifty feet long, were especially desirable and were traded up and down the coast.

With the introduction of commercially made boats and engines, the manufacture of canoes by the Southeast Alaska Indians almost disappeared. While other Northwest Coast Indians at the southern terminus started to reintroduce the traditional canoes in the late 1970s and 1980s, it wasn't until the late 1990s that the Tlingit and Haida began to make wooden canoes again. The traditional knowledge was almost lost, but a few artists were able to study under elders to regain the knowledge. In addition, three fiberglass canoes that closely followed the traditional designs were made.

In Celebration 2002, a group of young men organized canoe racing from Juneau to Douglas across the Gastineau Channel. By Celebration 2004, six teams that included both men and women entered the canoe race. Sponsors of Celebration had assisted with these events, but by Celebration 2006, Sealaska Heritage Institute assumed full responsibility for organizing the races. With the addition of the Juried Art Show and Competition and the Canoe Racing, Celebration had expanded to a five-day event.

Baby Regalia Review

Celebration 2006 marked the beginning of the Baby Regalia Review. It was an immediate success, with forty youngsters two years of age and under participating. The organizers declined to make the Baby Regalia Review competitive as they realized the impossibility of selecting one child over another as a winner. Instead, the Baby Regalia Review was an opportunity to introduce children to their culture and heritage. Of course, it was also seen as an occasion where proud parents and grandparents who accompany their children onstage could show their children and grandchildren dressed in the finest regalia made especially for them. Viewers across the state and nation are able to see the review, since Celebration is televised live throughout Alaska and can also be seen internationally through a webcast.

Each child participating in the Baby Regalia Review is introduced by his or her European and Native names. They are also introduced by their tribal and clan membership and the names of their parents and grandparents. Each item of their regalia and who made it is then described in great detail.

Each participant receives a certificate attesting to their participation in the Celebration Baby Regalia Review. Parents are also able to purchase a DVD of the event. The audience in the first Baby Regalia Review through their thunderous ovation made it clear that they would like to see this event continue.

Opposite: Celebration 2004.

Opposite: Parade. Left to right: Frank Jim wearing brown bear hide and *Teikweidí* (Brown Bear) *shakee.át* (frontlet headdress) with bear claws, Paul Willis (partially obscured) Steven Frank holding Raven dance staff, Reggie John wearing a Double-Headed Raven tunic and hat.

Left: Parade. David Katzeek (drumming) leads dancers through downtown Juneau.

Right: Parade. The parade goes on rain or shine. Left to right: Peter Marvin (wearing leather apron), Salina Thomas (drumming).

Below: Parade. Marie Beierly and baby react to Ben Coronell in a wolf headdress.

Celebration Events • 131

2006 Juried Art Show and Competition.
Thank You Halibut People Button Robe
by Chloe French.

2006 Juried Art Show and Competition.
Tsirku River Robe by Lani Hotch.
Second Place, Contemporary.

2006 Juried Art Show and Competition.
The Good Book by Nicholas Galanin.
First Place, Contemporary.

2002 Juried Art Show and Competition.
Tlingit Movement by Celeste Worl.

Celebration Events • 133

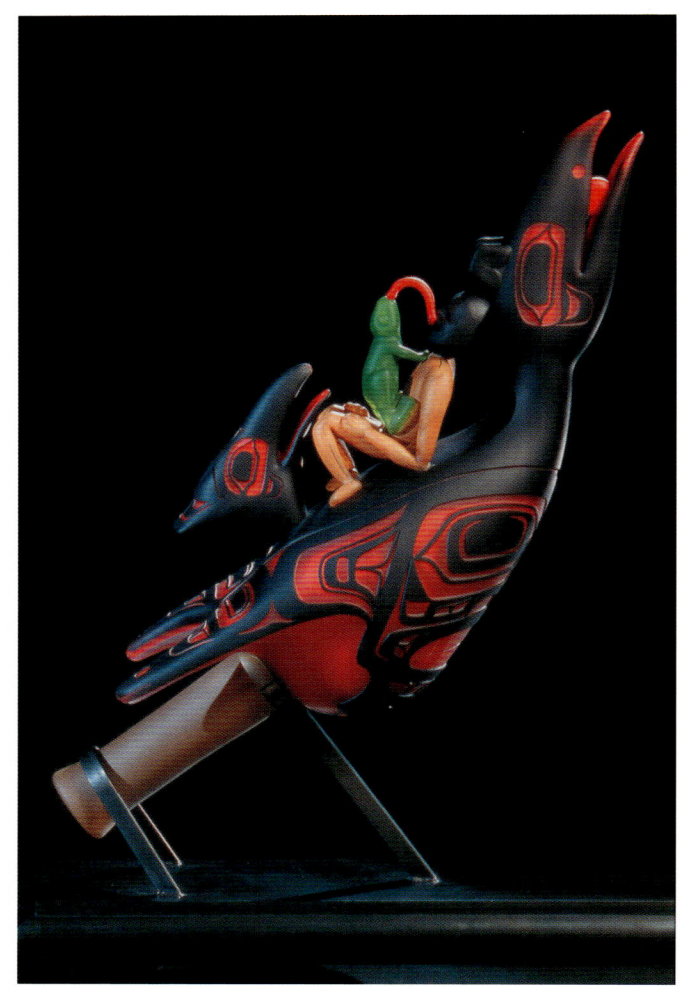

2004 Juried Art Show and Competition.
Raven Rattle by Preston Singletary.

2006 Juried Art Show and Competition.
Fooled You Again Raven Transformation
Mask by David A. Boxley.
First Place, Traditional.

2002 Juried Art Show and Competition.
Copper Woman by Clarissa Hudson.
Best of Show.

2002 Juried Art Show and Competition.
Raven Shakee.át by Archie Cavanaugh.

2004 Juried Art Show and Competition.
Raven's Dream Silver Spoon by William Pfeifer.
Third Place, Traditional.

Celebration Events • 135

2006 Juried Art Show and Competition.
Jeanine Clam Basket by Deborah Head.

Native Artist Market.
Killerwhale earrings by Richard Beasley.

Native Artist Market.
Chilkat doll by George Carteeti.

Native Artist Market.
Keeper of the Halibut halibut hook by Donald Gregory.

Native Artist Market.
Potlatch spoon by Clarence Jackson.

Native Artist Market.
Moccasins by Sarah Williams.

Celebration Events • 137

Left: Black Seaweed Contest. Seaweed entries are placed on numbered plates for sampling by judges, who are unaware of the contestants' identities.

Below: Canoe song. Dancers performing a canoe song and simulating paddle strokes. Far right: Paul Johnson of Angoon.

Below right: Canoe song. *Tuul Gundlaas Xyaal Xaadee* (Rainbow Creek) Dancers. Left to right: Ben Davidson (in back), Terri-Lynn Williams-Davidson (holding paddle).

138 • *Celebration*

Canoe race. One People team. Left to right: Roseanne Warner wearing turquoise vest, Rosalyn Cruise, Michael Chilton wearing turquoise vest, Mary Folleti (front), Ashli Hobbs (behind Mary).

Canoe race. Front: SouthEast Alaska Regional Health Consortium (SEARHC) team. Ben Joseph (short hair, red vest, middle), Rico Worl (in yellow), Gordon Guanzon (blue hood, white visor). The Devil's Club logo on the canoe signifies spiritual and physical strength. Rear: Tlingit Warriors team.

Celebration Events • 139

Baby Regalia Review. Jolynn Tripi with Renee Peck.

Baby Regalia Review. Bryson Andrew Mathias Jim with his mother, Ann Jim.

Far left: Baby Regalia Review. AJ Wilson.

Left: Baby Regalia Review. Cheyenne Jack Lafferty.

Above: Baby Regalia Review. Jazon Felix with his grandmother, Marilyn Boggs.

Celebration Events • 141

Clockwise from above: Baby Regalia Review. Helen Elizabeth John, Naomi Renee Miller, Kaden Dean Jim, Jossline Leighann Aranda-Jackson.

Far left: Baby Regalia Review. From left: Kahlyl Dybdahl held by grandfather Ed Hotch, with his granddaughter Larissa Lee Dybdahl.

Above: Baby Regalia Review. Four generations. Sophia Cadiente-Laiti-Blattner held by her mother, Dionne Cadiente-Laiti, and accompanied by her great-grandmother, Irene Cadiente (far left) and grandmother Andrea Cadiente-Laiti.

Left: Baby Regalia Review. Pietr Dabaluz.

Celebration Events • 143

Baby Regalia Review. *Clockwise from above:*

Kayaani Rae Weathers.

Micheel Martin (in wagon), Michaela Martin and Kahlyl Dybdahl (baby in white) with Michelle Martin (left).

Roberta Johnson holding her grandson, Jamaal Isaac Johnson.

Dasanial Joseph Dugaqua held by his mother, Kristy Dugaqua.

Far left: Baby Regalia Review. Atticus Baker.

Baby Regalia Review. Jamie Simone Quinto held by father, James Quinto.

Far left: Baby Regalia Review. Thomas S. George Barlow with his mother, Lisa George.

Baby Regalia Review. Sage Worl with his mother, Dawn Dinwoodie.

Celebration Events • 145

Baby Regalia Review. *Clockwise from above:*

Isabella Christine Hoppe with her mother Angela Hoppe.

Jordan Kelly Bennett with her father, Byron Jack, Jr.

Lelehua Fujimoto Vertido with her mother, Angel Fujimoto.

Jillian Hokland.

Baby Regalia Review. *From left:*
Aaron Handy.
Alexandra Bo Garcia.
Colin Patrick Rose.

Celebration Events • 147

Left: Baby Regalia Review. Asha Alana High runs behind Samual Logan White.

Below: Baby Regalia Review. Theodore Willard Guthrie II.

148 • *Celebration*

Left: **Baby Regalia Review. Gabrielle George-Frank.**

Below: **Baby Regalia Review. Left to right: Jordan Malea Casulucan, Joseph Casulucan, Taisun Julius, Hannahlynn Lee Kadinger (rear, with pacifier) with her mother, Louise Kadinger.**

Celebration Events • 149

Opposite: Grand exit. 2004.

Above: Grand exit. Gene Tagaban and Rangimarie Maori Dancers of New Zealand.

Right: Grand exit, 2004.

150 • *Celebration*

The Authors

ROSITA WORL (*Yeidiklas'akw Kwaa haní*) is Eagle (*Ch'áak'*) moiety of the Thunderbird (*Shangukweidí*) Clan from the House Lowered From the Sun (*Kawdliyaayi Hít*) in Klukwan. *Yeidiklas'akw* has a Ph.D. and a M.S. in anthropology from Harvard University, and a B.A. in social science from Alaska Methodist University. She wrote her doctoral dissertation on Tlingit property law. She serves as president of Sealaska Heritage Institute.

ROBERT DAVIDSON (*guud san glans*) is Haida of the Eagle moiety of the *t'saahl ʔlanaas* Clan. He is an internationally renowned artist and is recognized as one of Canada's most respected and important contemporary artists.

MARIA WILLIAMS (*Shaan Tláa*) is Tlingit of the Raven moiety of the *Deisheetaan* Clan. She is a child of the *Dakl'aweidí* of the *ÁaTlein Kwáan*. She is also Carcross-Tagish First Nations. *Shaan Tláa* received a Ph.D. in Music, specializing in ethnomusicology from UCLA. Her master's thesis was on Tlingit music, and her dissertation was on Alaska Native music and dance. She currently teaches at the University of New Mexico and spends summers in Alaska.

BYRON I. MALLOTT (*Dook da Naik*) is Tlingit of the Raven moiety of the *Kwaashk'i Kw'aan* Clan, of which he is the current Clan Leader. He was Sealaska Corporation's president and chairman during the first several Celebrations. During his presidency, the Sealaska Heritage Foundation (Institute) was established. He currently serves as a member of Sealaska's Board of Directors. He and his wife Toni (*Koyukon Athapascan*) raised their five children to know and live their Nativeness with pride.